innovation
you

innovation
YOU

FOUR STEPS TO BECOMING
NEW AND IMPROVED

Jeff DeGraff

Ballantine Books | New York

Published in the United States by Ballantine Books,
an imprint of The Random House Publishing Group,
a division of Random House, Inc., New York.

BALLANTINE and colophon are registered trademarks of Random House, Inc.

Library of Congress Cataloging-in-Publication Data
DeGraff, Jeffrey Thomas.
Innovation you : four steps to becoming new and improved / Jeff DeGraff.
p.   cm.
ISBN 978-0-345-53069-1 (hbk. : alk. paper) — ISBN 978-0-345-53070-7 (ebook)
1. Self-actualization (Psychology)   2. Creative ability.   3. Change (Psychology)
4. Career changes.   I. Title.
BF637.S4D435 2011
158.1—dc23   2011017710

Printed in the United States of America on acid-free paper

www.ballantinebooks.com

2 4 6 8 9 7 5 3 1

First Edition

Book design by Donna Sinisgalli

To my mother, Joan, who taught me to love words,
and to my father, Jim, who encouraged me to seek out the world.
They have been my guiding lights and I am most grateful
for their enduring love and support.

Special thanks to Debra Goldstein, G. F. Lichtenberg,
and Marnie Cochran, who made this book happen.

To my wife, Staney, the love of my life, for everything.

contents

Introduction   XIII

step I

RETHINK INNOVATION

chapter 1   CREATIVIZE   6

chapter 2   THERE IS NO DATA ON THE FUTURE—
WHERE WE GROW   12

chapter 3   YOU ARE NOT THE WEATHER   16

chapter 4   WE GROW WHEN OUR LIFE SUCKS . . .
OR WHEN WE'RE ON A ROLL   21

chapter 5   LIGHT YOUR FIRE WHERE THE SPARKS OF
DIVERSITY FLY   27

chapter 6   THE CAVALRY ISN'T COMING   31

chapter 7   RIDE WHAT MOVES   36

chapter 8   EFFICIENCY CAN KILL YOU—
THE 20–80 RULE   41

step II

REVISE YOUR APPROACH WITH PRISMATIC THINKING

chapter 9   THINK AROUND THE COLORS   50

chapter 10   STACK THE RUSSIAN NESTING DOLLS   64

chapter 11   HOW YOU INNOVATE IS WHAT YOU INNOVATE   73

chapter 12   THE MOST POWERFUL APPROACH TO
INNOVATION   80

chapter 13   CREATE CAPACITY—EMPTY THE BAG   86

chapter 14   AVOID THE NEGATIVE ZONE   92

step III

RUN YOUR EXPERIMENTS

chapter 15   COMMIT TO EXPERIMENT   105

chapter 16   HEDGE NOW, OPTIMIZE LATER   108

chapter 17   DECONSTRUCT TO RECONSTRUCT   113

chapter 18   SET HIGH-QUALITY TARGETS   115

chapter 19   ENLIST DEEP AND DIVERSE DOMAIN EXPERTISE   120

chapter 20   APPRENTICE THE SORCERER   124

chapter 21   MASTER SODOTO   127

chapter 22   TAKE MULTIPLE SHOTS ON GOAL   132

chapter 23   FAIL EARLY, FAIL OFTEN, FAIL OFF-BROADWAY   137

chapter 24   SHOW, DON'T TELL   141

chapter 25   YOU ARE THE STAR ONLY IN
YOUR OWN MOVIE   144

chapter 26   THE MONGOLIAN BARBECUE EFFECT   148

chapter 27   HIDE INSIDE TROJAN HORSES   150

chapter 28   LEARN FROM EXPERIENCE AND EXPERIMENTS   153

chapter 29   WHEN NOTHING SEEMS TO WORK   162

chapter 30   THINK IN TERMS OF CYCLES, NOT LINES   170

step IV

SEE THE WHOLE JOURNEY

chapter 31   WELCOME CREATIVE DESTRUCTION   179

chapter 32   WATCH FOR THE OFF-RAMPS AND ON-RAMPS   189

chapter 33   WE ALL HATE CHANGE   194

chapter 34   BUILD A PORTFOLIO LIFE   200

chapter 35   EXPECT RESISTANCE   213

chapter 36   THE GIFT   218

Appendix—Instructions for the Innovation You Assessment   223

introduction

One day it hits you: The game has changed. What always worked for you before, professionally or personally, no longer gets results. Maybe you lose a job or reach the end of a long relationship and you realize: *I'm done here—but this could be my chance for something better.* Maybe you hold on to that job, or meet your commitments to family, friends, and community, but underneath your success you feel: *This isn't enough. Not anymore, not at this time of my life.* At such moments, you know that both the game *and* you must change, and there's only one way forward: Innovate. Make it new. Make *you* new.

For so many people I meet, that moment has arrived. I think of Teri, a high school math teacher who had always secretly dreamed of becoming a baker. In the same week, she lost her teaching job to budget cuts and heard about a six-month sublease on a storefront downtown with good baking ovens. Her savings would just cover it. It was a big risk for her, but then again, this was what she'd always wanted. She asked me: "Should I go for my dream?"

Then there was Vago, who ran a successful financial advisory practice. He'd built his company by providing a unique service for high-net-worth investors, and as it grew he handpicked a circle of "disciples" who learned to do what he did. As the company expanded, each of the members of that circle hired his or her own circle. In theory, this meant that everyone in the company could provide the same excellent approach that Vago had first pioneered, but in recent years it had been more like photocopying the photocopy of a photocopy: The lines blurred and the quality was lost. Vago had begun to worry that his company's star was fading and that his best days were behind him. Was there a way to get back to the excitement and the success he'd known before?

Vago and Teri were in very different situations, but their basic life situation was the same: Their old approaches had stopped working and they were both trying to do something new. They had to do something they hadn't done before in a way they hadn't done it. And that's what it means to innovate. You don't know exactly where you're going, you don't know how to drive this kind of car, and you need to get there soon.

So how do you learn to innovate? These days, people from all walks of life come to me for individual guidance. Who am I? Why should you trust me to help renew and improve your life? I am one of the leading innovation experts you've never heard of . . . until now. I have been called "the Dean of Innovation" for my work with hundreds of the most recognized firms in the world, including American Airlines, Coca-Cola, General Electric, Pfizer, and Toyota, and my business writings are found in the playbooks for innovation programs at Thomson-Reuters, Johnson & Johnson, and other industry leaders. I headline conferences for everyone from Visa to the Federal Bureau of Investigation to Telemundo. I'm a top-rated professor at the prestigious Ross School of Business at the University of Michigan, and founder of the Innovatrium, a creativity lab where executives come from around the world to learn our proven scientific method and to jump-start innovation for corporate reinvention and growth.

Increasingly, I've found that my clients at the Innovatrium and my speaking audiences around the world are coming to me with something new: personal stories. And behind every story is the same urgent question: Jeff, you work with companies that continue to innovate, grow, and thrive, no matter how bad the weather gets out there. How can we do what they do?

How do you innovate you?

In this book, I show how it's done. Think of *Innovation You* as the key to your own personal Innovatrium, a private creativity lab where you will learn my four-step model for restoring growth and remaking your life. Here, I draw on twenty-five years of success with corporations of every kind, some in crisis, some broadening their ambitions, to show you how to innovate better so you can grow to reach your own goals—whether personal or professional.

This book is broken down into four sections, corresponding to the four steps our corporate clients take at the Innovatrium. Step I, "Rethink Innovation" shows you the opportunities to inject creativity into every aspect of your life. Step II, "Revise Your Approach with Prismatic Thinking," explains the four most common approaches to innovation, as established in a model of corporate growth that I codeveloped for business use, and that has become one of the most influential theories of organizational culture and competency. In this book, I've adapted that method for individuals. By making use of this tool, you will come to recognize which of these four approaches you commonly use to create value in your life, and what you *could* be doing if you understood the full range of your possibilities. In Step III, "Run Your Experiments" you learn to implement your freshly revised approach in the cycle of innovation. And in Step IV, "See the Whole Journey," you discover how ongoing success, whether for an individual or for a multinational corporation, depends on understanding and working with innovation's long-term cycles.

Guided by *Innovation You*, you will:

- Discover the mistaken assumptions that hold even creative people back.
- Recognize the approach to innovation you rely on without

thinking, and learn to craft a more effective approach to better reach your goals—even as conditions change around you.

- Identify practical methods for setting meaningful goals, overcoming resistance from yourself or those around you, and turning setbacks into vital discoveries.
- Reimagine innovation as a lifelong practice, so that personal growth never ends.

The recent severe recession has made personal innovation an urgent priority, not only for individuals but for companies and nations. I think of one Fortune 500 client, which I'll call Fortuna, whose ongoing success depended on a steady flow of new ideas and products. Executives at Fortuna called me because they discovered that their carefully planned processes and incentives had stopped working. Despite their system of offering "greenhouse funds," seed money for employees who wanted to test new projects, the money was just sitting in a bank account. No one was testing new ideas anymore. What had gone wrong?

Well, for one thing, the real estate market had collapsed. It was a Category 1 disaster. Employees at all levels were fearful for their jobs and upset about colleagues who had been laid off. Those remaining worked overtime to keep up with the increased workload they inherited. They felt too anxious and too pressured to devise or test new ideas. They only wanted to play it safe and hold on to their jobs.

What they didn't understand was that in the long term, playing it safe was the most dangerous thing they could do. It wouldn't lead to new ideas and new products, which were the future of the company—and their paychecks. Just as in the country as a whole, productivity at Fortuna was up, but it wasn't leading to growth. So I told them: You have to help your people see that in a down economy, innovation is not their best friend. It's their only friend. Things will not get better until the company has great new products to sell and in surprising new ways. You have to give your employees all the practical support and encouragement you can to help them believe that—and to innovate, today.

Three major business studies this year reached the same conclusion: The most urgent business need, according to separate researchers at IBM, Boston Consulting Group, and the Council on Competitiveness, is to develop the ability of each individual to find creative solutions to work challenges and to innovate for him- or herself. Although group innovation processes are important, they are not enough. According to a *Newsweek* cover article, the entire country is heading for a "creativity crisis." At the very moment when a survey of fifteen hundred CEOs named creativity the most important element for success in an increasingly complex world—ahead of rigor, management, discipline, integrity, and even vision—American children are scoring lower than ever on measures of creativity. Some blame the passive culture of video. Others point to the decline of creativity teaching in schools, from the gutting of art and music classes in elementary and high schools to the shift away from liberal and fine arts majors in college. For these and other reasons, this country is losing its edge in creativity when we need it most. That's the deeper crisis that inspired *Innovation You*—and the deeper opportunity for you to bring the full benefits of creativity into your life, no matter what you hope to do next.

Let me start to show you how it works. Recall Teri, who lost her full-time teaching job and who saw a chance to turn that job loss into a dream come true. The risk was big. Should she invest the bulk of her savings in a sublease on a bakery storefront? I told her she should definitely go for her dream, but that in my model of innovation, before you make specific commitments for achieving any goal, you first rethink your overall approach. Teri had been a very good teacher because she was devoted, organized, and efficient with her time. She returned her students' work quickly, with detailed comments so they could learn from their mistakes. She devised systems on her computer for tracking her students' progress. Of the four basic approaches to innovation, she was what we call a red or "Control" innovator, one whose approach creates value by increasing productivity while doing things correctly.

But was the approach from her previous project—teaching—going to suit this new one? Were bakery customers like high school students? Was baking like the math curriculum? Unlike students, customers are not required to come to your bakery when the bell rings. A baker has to learn what will draw customers in and make them feel like coming back. And unlike mathematics, baking has no fixed curriculum, with algebra leading to pre-calculus and then to calculus. There was no one right answer about what to bake or what style to make it in—success required getting to know her customers and their preferences, a subtle kind of teamwork that takes time. In my terms, as I'll explain in Step II, Teri needed to blend her "Control" approach with a "Collaborate" approach, something that was new to her.

The risk for Teri in renting a storefront now was that in six months, she might still be getting to know the local customers, perfecting her recipes, and building her reputation. If she committed all of her savings now, she would have nothing left if she needed more time. I suggested she look for an approach that would give a year or even two in which to blend her old "Control" approach with the "Collaborate" demands of her new career.

She decided to take on some substitute-teaching work to pay the bills while continuing to bake at home. She found a local restaurant willing to feature some of her home-baked goods—and let her discover the reactions they got from real customers. She set up a weekly table at the local farmer's market. Then she realized that her connections in the public school system gave her access to people who made the purchasing decisions for her old school's cafeteria and fund-raising events. In all of these ways, she joined forces with other existing institutions and individuals, as a way to get to know her "audience" while building a reputation with them. She shifted her approach to do more collaboration and more learning. She avoided a potentially disastrous mistake—betting all of her resources on a single attempt—and instead developed the expertise and partnerships that gave her the best chance to succeed in her dream of becoming a baker.

For Vago, the question wasn't how to build something from scratch, it was how to reinvigorate a fading success. How could he keep his company growing when it had outgrown his model for growth? I started with the principle "How You Innovate Is What You Innovate." Vago had always grown the company in one way: by finding people who could deliver the company's expertise just as he did. I asked him if he had ever considered other approaches. What if he expanded instead by partnering with others who had their own complementary kinds of expertise? Or what if he increased his reach by making some services available over the Internet rather than in personal consultations?

Normally, as I help clients generate new ideas with the principles in this book, they get excited. But Vago didn't seem excited. He seemed increasingly hesitant. There had been a time early on in his career, he finally told me, when he had tried many different approaches. But back then he didn't have much to lose. Now, though, he had a reputation to preserve—and a client base to maintain. He couldn't just take a trusting client and experiment on him or her in the name of "innovation."

As he voiced his fear, I realized that his way of *thinking about* innovation was preventing him from *doing* it. So I turned the conversation to another of the principles you'll find in this book: "Fail Early, Fail Often, and Fail Off-Broadway." The only way to develop good innovations is to test a lot of attempts to find out what works—and what doesn't. This means that the goal is not to prevent failures but rather to fail more and faster, and to do it in safe, out-of-the-way places. Just as Broadway shows used to have their first run in New Haven or even Chicago in order to keep any early problems out of sight of the big audiences and the influential theater critics in New York City, I suggested that Vago try out new approaches on smaller clients who might be interested in something new. Then if those new approaches didn't work as hoped, he could be confident they wouldn't affect his relationships with his best clients.

This approach gave Vago one of the things he'd lost when he became a success—a safe place to fail. He took on some smaller clients he might otherwise have turned away, clients who were interested in sampling a new approach. He offered them the choice of one of three tiers of service, inspired by the American Express green, gold, and platinum cards. Success with these "off-Broadway" clients convinced Vago to offer his new suite of products to all of his clients, with different advisers assigned to handle different levels of service. In this way he could narrow what he asked of his employees, increase overall quality, and revive his business. With these innovations, his company began to grow again.

As these examples show, I may be a professor, but at heart I'm more like a football coach. I want to show you where to run and how to make your moves, explaining where all the X's and O's go in the play diagram so you can get out on the field with a new way to win. I love big thinking, but I believe that after all the learning, you have to *deliver*. Despite piles of business and self-help books, no one has provided a step-by-step playbook for reinventing yourself as the game changes. But with *Innovation You*, I'll show you how.

step I

RETHINK INNOVATION

Life can only be understood backwards;
but it must be lived forwards.
—Søren Kierkegaard

At first, it seemed like a dream assignment. A friend of mine at Reuters whom I'll call Andrew was tapped to develop new information products for the emerging Indian market. India is a huge country, with a growing economy, a vast population, and increasing technological sophistication. However, as he got to know the country, Andrew realized that the vast majority of small business owners in India didn't have the money to buy existing Reuters products. They could not afford the dedicated terminals that received data feeds. Many of them could not even afford a laptop computer. He also discovered that he had been given only a small budget for developing new products, so he couldn't afford to innovate in the usual Reuters way, hiring market researchers and a product development team. In short, he couldn't afford to develop new products and his customers couldn't afford the existing ones. His dream job was beginning to seem like a nightmare.

Andrew couldn't increase his budget or change his potential customers, so he had only two choices: accept defeat or innovate. He began to look more closely at each of the elements available to work with. He traveled to markets in different Indian cities, talking to the farmers he found there, and he discovered that they shared a common problem. When they took their goods to market, they got ripped off. Farmers would load up their trucks with vegetables and then face a choice: Which market would pay the best price? They had no way to get information about prices offered in different cities, and the wholesalers who bought their wares knew the farmers were in the dark. So the wholesalers set prices low, confident that the farmers couldn't afford to drive from city to city to find the best price.

This was a problem that Reuters' information could solve—as part of their existing products, they offered vast amounts of commodity pricing information. But these farmers didn't care about the whole range of commodities. They only cared about prices for farm products. At first, that seemed like more bad news: Here was a pool of potential "customers" who had no money to buy Reuters products *and* no interest in what they sold. But on reflection, my colleague realized that wasn't quite right. It wasn't that these farmers had no money and no interest—they had a small amount of money and a highly focused interest in the commodities they grew. That was something he could work with.

Andrew realized he could make a new product by breaking off a little piece of the existing product, Reuters Market. Instead of selling a complete commodities information subscription, he would sell just the farm prices that interested them, along with weather information and advice for farmers on when to plant and when to harvest. Instead of sending the information over the Internet, which many farmers couldn't access, he offered it by text to their cellphones. And instead of charging the full price for a full commodities subscription, he charged a small fraction of the price for a small fraction of the information.

The product, named Reuters Market Light, proved extremely valuable to farmers. The weather and farming advice increased their yields, and the pricing information gave them leverage in their price negotiations. News of the product quickly spread by word of mouth, and though profit on each subscription was tiny, the market proved to be vast. Reuters Market Light was a success made possible by the new understanding of how the information "game" had to be played in India and by the small, creative changes made in several aspects of a product they already had.

How did Andrew find this opportunity, and ultimately this success, one he might easily have missed? He "creativized." Creativizing means finding a new solution not by throwing away an old solution and starting over, but by looking at each piece of the current situation and making small, creative changes part by part, experimenting along the way. It requires thinking differently about your overall situation, both bad and good, and the ways that you can respond to that situation. At heart, it means thinking differently about innovation: what it is and what sort of mental stance you need to do it well. So here in Step I, we focus on developing the mental stance of the innovator, which is the crucial—but often overlooked—first step in the cycle of innovation.

chapter one

CREATIVIZE

Henry Martin is important to me for what may seem a humble reason. A chemist in Buffalo, New York, in the mid-twentieth century, Martin changed dry cleaning forever when he created a cleaning solvent that wouldn't burst into flames. Until 1949, the storefronts that people called "dry cleaners" were only pick-up and drop-off sites. The chemicals used to clean clothes were so dangerous that the actual cleaning had to be done in the safety of a factory, where a fire could be contained. But Martin's nonflammable solvent meant that dry cleaning could be done where the customers were. This new approach, "Martinizing," saved customers days of waiting and gave Martin's stores an advantage over every competitor.

In a similar way, the first step toward innovating your own life is to look for the opportunities to add creativity to each element of what you do—not just sending out for creativity like the old dry cleaners used to send out their clothes to the factory, but adding in creativity yourself where you live and work. Martinizing made dry cleaning safe, ordinary, everyday—and hugely successful. That's what creativity needs to be in your life.

The innovation visionary Marshall McLuhan made the point that innovation is not a thing. It's an attribute or quality: An innovation is anything that is enhanced—made better or new. To see what

I mean, pick up any business magazine. You are likely to find examples of the most innovative companies in the world. But look a little closer and you will find that some of these businesses excel at marketing, while others excel at technology development, and yet others don't seem to do anything revolutionary, but they are great at increasing revenues. The point is that these examples are all over the place, because innovation is something you can do in different forms, at different times, in different places. If it makes your business (or your life) better relative to your own idea of what better would be, it's an innovation. Sometimes the biggest innovations are actually steps backward into the past, like the local food movement, in which well-off people with access to a global transportation network that can bring them food from anywhere in the world try as hard as they can to eat the food grown right nearby, as farming people did when there were no planes, trains, or automobiles.

Innovation is any creative improvement, and "creativizing" can improve any area of your life. Shandra creativized when she received an unexpected medical diagnosis: Cancer. Aggressive tumors. Odds no better than fifty-fifty. All she could think at first was, *This wasn't supposed to happen.* She had lived through a difficult divorce and was raising three children on her own. After years of night school and crummy jobs, she had found a position at a company that saw the good in her. She had advanced quickly to become an executive secretary. Now everything she had built for her family, from the condo in the good school district to the college tuition savings accounts to the possibility of retiring to watch over future grandchildren was all at risk.

The doctor spoke compassionately and made his recommendations. A patient like this should start chemotherapy right away. He offered a list of support groups to help with the emotional strain. Yet Shandra felt she'd been given a death sentence. When she finally got home, she couldn't bear to speak to her children. She paid the sitter, made her way upstairs, and climbed into bed.

The next day, Shandra went to a support group of cancer patients in treatment, but it only made her feel more afraid and helpless. Resigned to her fate, she called her family together. There was a long silence after the announcement. Finally her oldest daughter spoke up. "You taught all of us that anything may be possible as long as we were willing to take responsibility for giving our best," she said. "I want to believe you're due for a miracle. We are here with you to help you in any way we can."

After that emotional homecoming, the family pulled together. If conventional medicine only gave Shandra a fifty-fifty chance, what alternatives could they find? If the support group wasn't enough, where could she find even more support? Together they began making phone calls, searching the Internet, reading books, and holding regular kitchen-table conclaves. They knew the cancer was not in their control, but few situations are. Together they set out to do what innovators everywhere try to do: improve the odds, both for a good outcome and for a better experience for Shandra, no matter what happened.

The following week, Shandra visited a few different specialists, including Dr. Li, who was highly regarded for both conventional and Eastern medical practices. In his office, she took a seat near the comforting babble of a tranquillity fountain. The attendant brought an elegant tea tray. Then the doctor pulled up a chair and quietly introduced himself. He explained his approach of partnering with patients because only they really know what their body needs.

At the next kitchen-table gathering, Shandra said she believed that Dr. Li could help her find her own way to healing. Along with regular checkups and a regimen of chemotherapy, the program would include meditation, Chinese herbal remedies, and daily Qigong exercises. The treatment was disruptive and hard to endure. At the start of each session with Dr. Li, Shandra would relate which treatments she thought were working and which were not. The doctor weighed her impressions as he adjusted her program week by week.

She found meditation helpful but wanted to add some traditional prayers, as well as ones she had written, to incorporate her deep faith.

Months later, after follow-up tests, Dr. Li announced that Shandra showed no more traces of the disease. He cautioned her to remain ever vigilant and wished her well. She was deeply grateful and returned to work, but now devoted time each day to the regimen she had created to maintain her health.

Shandra was fortunate, but she had also done what she could to create her own good luck by approaching her challenge like a master innovator. Her first doctor had offered her the standard "recipe"—chemotherapy, a hospital-based support group, and waiting. But Shandra went beyond the standard approach. What I admired so much was not that she tried alternative medicine—lots of people do that—but that she found ways to add her own creativity at *every* step. She took her doctor's advice but added her own research as well. She joined the hospital's support group but also established a second support group from her community of family and friends. She took the conventional Western medical approach and added Eastern medicine. She prayed, which had always been a support for her, but she added meditation and visualization, techniques she had never tried. For every element of her treatment, she added new, creative ingredients and methods. She "creativized."

People who don't creativize may never know what they're missing. The price of not creativizing comes in missed opportunities to grow and thrive, but if you miss those opportunities you may have no way to know what, specifically, was lost. Had Reuters not created Reuters Market Light, the company might never have realized that its international sales were far below their potential. They only found answers by improvising. They only discovered the possibility of success by creating it.

How? The key to creativizing is to open up your thinking to see your true situation and your range of possible responses in the widest possible way. Most people facing a crisis or opportunity will start out with an idea or two about what's wrong and what they could do differently. They'll probably deny the situation for as long as they can. Then maybe they'll get a little advice. If they're not desperate, they'll probably procrastinate. When they finally do feel desperate, they often leap at any chance that comes along.

But when you creativize, the goal is to see a much wider range of possibilities. This takes some courage, because to begin, you have to take an honest look at where things stand now. Often—not always, as we'll see, but often—things look pretty grim. Your old methods have stopped working and you have no guarantees about what could take their place. The weather is threatening. You're already working hard. It may feel like you have no options at all. No one is coming to save you. So what can you do? Look around, and keep your eyes open. Find out what exactly are the threats that require you to innovate. Where are the new areas of growth that could sustain you and improve your life? How are your assumptions about creativity holding you back? What is keeping you from finding the people and the trends that can help you make the changes you need?

These are the questions we'll address here in Step I. It's a preparatory step, in which you develop the skills and habits you will need on your innovation journey. By the time you reach Step II, you may feel that instead of seeing too few options for achieving any specific change you would like in your life, now you will be creativizing too many. I hear this from my business students sometimes. We look at a case together and I start asking questions they don't expect. I talk about people and factors that weren't mentioned in the case. And they say: Wait! You're creating too many options! It feels like chaos.

I tell them: No, it's not chaos. It's possibility. This is what it feels like when you take off the blinders and see possibility all around. You don't have to follow up on every single one. In fact, later on in this process we'll learn ways to winnow and to test the possibilities to find the ones that are worth your while to test. But as you begin to creativize, if you feel overwhelmed with possibility, good. So many people start to change when they feel that life has backed them into a corner or when they feel tapped out of ideas or energy or are at a loss. Only when you realize you're *surrounded* by possibility— practical, start-today possibility—will you be ready for the later parts of the book, which guide you to select the *best* overall approach for reaching your goals, and then to find the specific methods that will turn your new approach into satisfying results.

chapter two

―――――

THERE IS NO DATA ON THE FUTURE — WHERE WE GROW

A journalist asked me, "Is the euro going to go up or down?"

"Up, of course," I said. That got his attention.

"Why?"

"Because it's down now. That's what currencies do. They go up and down."

"When?" he wanted to know. "When is it going to go up?"

All I could do was smile. "If I knew that, I wouldn't be telling you. I'd be off buying euros."

We would all like to know right away which of our ideas for how to make our lives better is going to succeed and which isn't, so we can be perfectly certain of success. That's why people buy so many of those checklist-type books with titles like *Seven Steps to Get Rich Quick*. We'd all love to find a foolproof checklist that will succeed everywhere, for everyone, forever—but as we find out sooner or later, there's no way to get that kind of perfect information. Just watch any old science fiction movie. It may be good or bad, but with hindsight we always find that the filmmaker never gets the future right. If you watch *2001: A Space Odyssey*, you'll see that the story assumed that by 2001 there would be two bases on the moon, one run by the United States and one by the Soviet Union. At the same time, when a character in the movie makes a video phone call, he has to sit inside a phone booth and pay by the minute—the creators were able to imagine an American moon base but not a free Internet phone call on a handheld device. And although it's supposed to be the future, everyone is dressed in closely tailored 1960s clothes because that's what was in style when the movie was made. There is no data on the fashion future, either.

Even graduates of business school fall into the trap of thinking they can know what the future will bring. MBAs typically try to understand the future by doing more research on the past, so they can document and repeat what worked before. But as innovators know, the game keeps changing. What worked before won't necessarily work again. There is no certainty. If you don't believe me, go read the checklist-style business books on innovation that were popular five years ago. Innovative business practices that were heralded as the next new thing are no longer applicable to handle current challenges.

Take a business practice called Total Quality Management. It was the innovative management approach developed back when the Japanese were suddenly making cars of much higher quality than we were making in America. Our cars were full of defects, and lots of Americans started to buy Japanese. To become competitive again, the Total Quality Management approach said that everyone involved in making a product like a car, including people outside the company, such as suppliers and customers, had to participate in checking and maintaining quality. It was a very good idea about how companies could make fewer mistakes, and by about the year 2000, American quality ratings were indistinguishable from those of Asian companies. TQM worked.

The trouble was, too many businesspeople forgot that TQM was an innovation developed to solve a specific problem at a specific time. They forgot that their fabulous data about TQM only applied to the past and that there was no data from the future. TQM came to be seen as a cure-all, a required "improvement" for any company. But eliminating errors is not the only thing companies have to do well. In fact, while American car companies were focusing increasingly on reducing the number of mistakes they made, Japanese and Korean companies shifted focus. They started to ask: How can we build exciting new luxury cars? How can we break into what has always been an American and European market? They had shifted from reducing errors to expanding into new markets, and the fact that American companies were hyperfocused on reducing manufacturing errors meant that Asian companies had plenty of time and room to innovate—and pull ahead of American manufacturers again.

All those American companies were making the same basic mistake: They thought that past success was a guarantee of future success. They didn't look for the next innovation. They bet it all on TQM. We all do this at times. Every year, it seems, as college admissions news comes in, I hear about some family shocked that their child hasn't gotten into any college except a safety school. They say something like: "How could that happen to Billy? He was such a smart little boy. Why, when he was four years old . . ." They're still relying on the mental picture they have of him from years ago—and ignoring more recent potential pictures, like the one of his school performing worse each year against local, state, and national benchmarks, or the one of smart Billy, bored in his failing school, cutting classes and getting into trouble.

embrace uncertainty

If past performance can't predict the future, and you can't rely on the methods that worked yesterday to work again for you tomorrow, then what can you do? How do you meet the uncertainty of the future—the only place where you can grow? By taking the mental stance of the successful creativizer. Neither hiding from change nor lost in endless preparation and research. Uncertain—but not upset to be uncertain. Because life can't be fully plotted in advance, only understood in hindsight, the innovator goes forward, uncertain but curious, interested, and responsive to new data as it comes in, and comes in again tomorrow. To grow requires that we temporarily suspend our need for certainty and control. Like plotting a journey on a map of a country we have never visited, we may be certain where our journey starts and pretty sure where we want to go, but we can't know what happens in between. Even though we can draw a straight line on the map from start to finish, we should know at the start that our journey won't follow that straight line. Roads wind, tides shift; there is rough weather to avoid and danger to overcome.

Innovation, at best, is a work in progress. We need to have a plan but also to practice what Saint Paul called "prudence." I'd summarize it this way: *I have a map, and I believe in the route that I have planned, but I may change my mind about which road to take when I see what's over the next hill.* Think about getting married. The gal or fellow you wind up with is always going to be different from the one you set out to find, and he or she will continue to change as the weather and the world change around you both. The same goes for a new job, an entire industry, your friendships, relationships to spiritual communities, and any other important part of your life. So I'm not saying that you can innovate to succeed in the long run. I'm saying that you can *only* succeed in the long run if you innovate and keep innovating, which means tolerating the uncertainty of the future. And that's part of the glory of it. Growth requires that we move out of the known and toward the unknowable, experimenting and revising as we go.

chapter three

———

YOU ARE NOT THE WEATHER

Like most children growing up in Michigan, I heard my mother tell me: *Watch the weather.* Our state has eleven thousand lakes and touches four of the five Great Lakes. The prevailing winds can shift suddenly from southwest to northwest. When hot weather blows across a Great Lake, the heat condenses into rain and suddenly you have a thunderstorm. When cold weather crosses a warmer lake, you get tornadoes. And during the winter, when cold water crosses over the lake, you get blizzards, Alberta Clippers. The weather is powerful and it changes fast; conditions quickly become dangerous, and it's not enough to notice that the sky has changed color. You need to respond.

For me, this childhood training served as a kind of inoculation against careless self-help optimism, the kind that says we can control everything just by "attracting" it with our thoughts. It also helped me learn the limits of psychological assessments such as the Myers-Briggs that categorize people into "types." I may be the adventurous type who dances in the rain or the practical type who wears galoshes, but in a hurricane it won't really matter what I'm wearing on my feet. What will matter is whether I know how to find shelter.

In the same way, even if you've got the perfect psychological profile to be a teacher, when there are no teaching jobs, you're going to have to work against type. To succeed, you have to pay attention to the weather: Check with the National Weather Service or look at what the beetles and birds are doing, and respond creatively. In this sense, my mother was giving me an early education in philosophy. Like Plato in the *Phaedrus*, she was telling me: You have a boat and you're on the ocean and you have a compass and sail and mast, but you are not the ocean. You didn't make this world. You're not half as powerful as certain New Age writers want you to think you are. There are forces bigger than you. So your goal is to recognize them, respect them, honor them—and go out and engage them with your own creativity. You may be the best passing quarterback there is, but if you're playing in the pouring rain, you better run the ball.

watch the weather

Don't most people notice the weather? Yes, but they don't respond to it. In my home state of Michigan, there were signs as far back as the 1970s that the auto manufacturing jobs on which so many relied were leaving the country. By 1994, Michael Moore had made *Roger and Me*, his movie about the horrific effects of outsourcing on his hometown of Flint. Word was out. I personally had two friends who took it upon themselves to get new training before their manufacturing jobs disappeared. They started to ask themselves and their friends: Is there any reason to think the number of auto factory jobs is going to go back up again? Is the work I do so special that it will be necessary no matter what happens to the auto industry?

When they thought about these questions, they realized the answers were no and no. So then they looked around for industries where the weather was better. Online sales were growing every year, and one of my friends had always liked and been good with computers. The population of elderly people in Michigan was growing, and my other friend—a big, burly guy, the last person you would have guessed—had always had a feeling for caring for the elderly. In the end, one became a website designer and the other a nurse. Yet most people with jobs in the auto industry kept going to work as if they didn't see the storm clouds or feel the first drops of rain. Either they felt the sensations and didn't think about them or they had no way to apply their creativity to what they observed all around.

How can you shift from passive notice of the weather to active response? To begin, make time to reflect on the larger changes going on around you. Instead of using all of your time to check items off the to-do list or kick back and relax, give yourself half a day a month, or two hours here and there, to watch the weather. Put it on your calendar. Treat it as one of your most important meetings. When the time comes, learn about changes going on in your area and your industry. How could you start?

- Read a news magazine or industry publication that you normally skip.
- Replace an hour of "entertainment" television each week with a news or documentary program about an issue you are concerned about.
- Browse an online news aggregator, such as Huffington Post or Google News, that gives a wide range of experts and observers a place to comment on the trends they observe.
- Make use of the expertise and experience of the people all around you. Make a point to talk to different folks at community gatherings—at a party, after religious services, at a school event—and ask them what's new in their business or their neighborhood. Where do they see opportunities? What has them concerned?
- When you travel, talk to the people traveling alongside you: the person next to you on the bus or plane, or in the seat nearby when you stop for a bite to eat; the driver of

the airport shuttle or the taxi. Are things changing around here? What's on their minds?

- Join a group on Facebook or another social networking site that provides neutral information on big-picture issues that concern you, such as health, education, or finance. Remember that the goal here is to choose a group that will expose you to new points of view, not just reinforce the views you expect to be true.

- If you have children in your life, discuss issues of the day that get raised at your child's school. Work to help your children develop a big-picture perspective. As you help them to think for themselves, you may find that they are learning things or encountering situations that are new to you as well.

In any of these ways, you can begin to become aware of the changes on the horizon. But don't just do this alone—find others who are interested in watching the weather and discussing the longer-term possibilities. "I saw on Huffington Post that X and Y. Do you think that will happen here?" "I read in the newspaper that . . ." Start an ongoing conversation with others and with yourself. Conduct thought experiments: When you look up at the sky, what do you see coming? What might that mean? Is that something that's going to matter for you?

The most important thing is to remember that you are starting a learning process that will take time. If you spend one afternoon learning and talking, chances are you won't end the day with any answers at all. That's exactly where you should be. For now, your goal is to establish the innovator's habit of looking up and identifying some clouds you need to keep an eye on, some areas down the road that are expecting sunshine. Throughout this book, we'll return to ways of watching the weather. It's a practice that may require a kind of innovation in your own perspective. To begin, I want to introduce an innovator's mantra: *Look up, down, and around.* Develop the habit of looking away from the life right in front of you, to see what else is coming your way. This is how you begin a longer process of exploration and discovery.

chapter four

·

WE GROW WHEN OUR LIFE SUCKS . . .
OR WHEN WE'RE ON A ROLL

Newcomers to an Alcoholics Anonymous meeting are often surprised that what you'll find there is the opposite of reassurance. Normally, if someone has a crisis, a friend will say: Relax, it's going to be okay, don't be too hard on yourself. Stay positive. Breathe. But at an AA meeting you have to stand up in front of everyone and say: Alcohol wrecked my life. Here's the painful story, and what am I today? I'm still an alcoholic.

This approach is a speed ramp to remembering the worst times, your most disappointing and shameful defeats. Why? When life is all right, it's comfortable to stay where you are and painful to commit to something new. Most of the time, we all strive for consistency and comfort: We want tomorrow to be reliably like today. That's why AA doesn't go easy on the novices: They understand that until newcomers own up to the reality of their situation, there is little hope of their kicking the habit. Yet when life feels miserable, risk and reward reverse: Now it hurts to stay where you are, but trying something new actually feels better. As Bob Dylan put it, "When you ain't got nothin', you got nothin' to lose."

We seldom change on our own. But most people will try something new—like not drinking even though they badly want a drink—if they feel bad enough. It's as true for companies as it is for individuals: Why is Apple doing well now? Because they nearly went bankrupt in 1997. They had to try a lot of risky, potentially embarrassing innovations because the alternative was to give up and go home. Out of those risks came the iPod, iTunes, the iPhone, and the iPad. We see this pattern over and over in business: The original vision of a hybrid engine like the one in the Prius was developed in the 1970s during the oil crisis. When gas prices came down, the idea got lost, but during the recession of 2008–9, when General Motors had to take a government bailout, they took the risk on finally producing the Volt, their hybrid. It's as Rahm Emanuel, President Obama's first chief of staff, liked to say: "A crisis is too valuable to waste."

We experience these same dynamics as individuals. Divorce, bankruptcy, and loss of health drive us into changes we previously believed unimaginable. We change, and hopefully grow, when our life sucks. When it comes to creativizing, if you want to move from idea to action, find the worst part of your life and focus on it. Where is the pain so high that trying something new would be an improvement? Remind yourself of what's wrong, and take an action there.

get on a roll

Is there no alternative to suffering in order to change and grow? Actually, there is. We are also freed to change when life exceeds our expectations. Graduation, a new job, true love, and the birth of a child are some of the events that make us feel like we're "on a roll." Economists call this "risk capital." When we're doing well, we know that even if something goes wrong, we can absorb the losses, so we take more risks because we know we won't be wrecked by a failure. I suspect this is one reason New Year's resolutions are so popular: Almost everyone feels at least a temporary feeling of optimism on New Year's Eve. That optimism makes contemplating change less painful.

At its best, getting on a roll is a feeling like invincibility—anyone who's been in love knows this feeling. It's also one reason the rich get richer—they can afford to take chances. But that doesn't mean only the rich and the newly in love can benefit. I think of Earl, who worked in the office cafeteria of a big company. His hours were long and his job did not offer much stimulation. When he first took the job, he thought it was a plus that there was always food available to him, but after a few years he weighed over three hundred pounds and he was having weight-related health problems.

One day Earl decided to make use of the company workout room. It was open to all employees, but I don't think he'd ever been down there before. I was part of a group of executives and business professors who worked out together on Thursdays. We all looked at Earl as he walked in. He was a big guy, tall, but he looked down at his shoes like a discouraged child. You could just feel how uncomfortable he felt. I remember him standing there in athletic clothes that didn't fit him well, and it was easy to imagine how this could go wrong in a couple of different ways: Here's a guy already self-conscious, with low self-esteem, who comes into this place for the first time, feels alone, feels he doesn't belong. Would he ever come back? Maybe he would sabotage himself by doing too much—he looked like the kind of guy who could wind up having a heart attack on the floor of the workout room.

Earl got on a treadmill and started to walk. One of the senior people in the company was working out next to him, an outgoing guy who'd had a career in the army before he went into business, and he started to chat with Earl. He said, "You're from food services, right? Great seeing you down here." Once he started talking to Earl, others joined in: "We treadmill every Thursday. If you want to come, join us."

Over the next few weeks, I saw him working out regularly. He didn't overdo it. First, he started by walking on the treadmill. After a few weeks of walking, he started to alternate walking and running.

A couple of months in, he added some time on the elliptical machine. He had a plan for his workouts, but then lots of people have workout plans that never amount to anything. After the holidays we all joked about how we'd fallen off the wagon, but there he still was. Week after week, he chose to work out when we did. We'd all see him and we'd encourage him, just as we supported each other: Great to see you again. Looking good!

One day I was down at the gym and he weighed in ahead of me. I said, "Earl! Wow! How much weight have you lost?"

"Fifty-five pounds."

"You didn't go on a big diet, did you?" I asked. I'd seen him in the cafeteria and to my eye he hadn't been starving himself.

"I'm not denying myself anything," he said. Instead, he'd gotten on a roll that first day, with a welcome and some encouragement where he probably wasn't expecting it, and he just kept developing his new approach to health. And I thought: *He's doing it*. He's innovating his own approach back to health. He's going to wind up a fit, two-hundred-pound guy because he got on a roll with people around him who encouraged him and then he used that energy to augment his own dedication and willpower. That encouragement seemed to lift some of the embarrassment and boredom that no doubt goes with making that kind of change in your life. So he developed more momentum. He smiled more, and he didn't look at his shoes as much. Now he was seeing the improvement, and that improvement kept him feeling he was on a roll. That's how winners continue to win.

In a way, it doesn't matter if things are going very well or very badly—on either side of normal comfort, there is the opportunity to launch an innovation. The problem is that people often pick the precisely wrong moment, when things are neither very good nor very bad. After New Year's Eve fades and you're back to the regular winter work routine, it's unlikely any resolution will stick—you're not in pain and you're not on a roll. What's more effective is to use New Year's Eve to review the past year and reconsider your goals. Collect some ideas of what would benefit you in the next year. Then wait for those moments when you feel either that you can't stand it any longer or that you can do anything—and pounce. That's the time to begin to put your resolution into practice. Be on the lookout for times when risk and reward reverse.

Say, for example, that you've had trouble on and off with back pain, or in fact with any sort of physical discomfort. Perhaps you've had the thought of seeing a chiropractor regularly or trying a gentle yoga class once or twice a week. Many people will do some research and then try to shoehorn such an activity into their ordinary life: From now on I'll go to yoga twice a week! Then they find that they don't stick with it. They start to feel guilty and that makes them even less likely to continue.

When *are* you likely to stick with such a plan? Either when you are in so much pain that you feel you have to do *something*, or when you've been feeling comfortable and free to do the things you love doing, and it comes to you: *This is great—and I want to hold on to it!* The key is to creativize regularly, so that you have possibilities in mind when the opportunity arises. Then, be on the lookout for the moments when risk and reward reverse and it feels good to try something new.

Here's an example. Clio had moved to Boston when she was on a roll. Not long after she'd fallen in love with a Bostonian, she was offered a great job there as well. Saying yes was easy—her new life felt less like a decision than a gift from above. But six years later, her situation had changed. The job was a great success and Clio became the second most important person in the company, but the head of the company felt threatened and began to fight her on issues large and small. The man she hoped to marry refused to commit and seemed to be slowly drifting away. Clio's mother was diagnosed with incurable cancer. For two years, her life became increasingly difficult. The gray Boston winters made her feel lonely and old. Her solace was hiking vacations in the Southwest. While on vacation she sent back postcards to friends in Boston that read, "I want to live here!" Clio's mother needed her close by, and she still held out hope for the relationship that had first brought her to Boston. Making a big change felt far too risky. She returned to her usual life.

The next year, Clio's mother passed away. Around the same time, she hired a personal coach to help her get out of her increasingly frustrating career rut. This time, when she returned from a vacation in the Southwest, she told her coach that she saw another option: The big companies in her industry were all in the Northeast, but there were smaller companies in need of experienced guidance. She began to fantasize about starting over as a consultant, living in a place that got three hundred days of sunshine a year. With her mother gone, and both her relationship and her job increasingly frustrating, she was miserable—but she also felt, for the first time, that she had much less to lose, and more to gain, by trying something new. Her coach said to her, "You know, you could take the initiative." She decided to go back to the Southwest, to scout for clients and possible places to live. Risk and reward had reversed again, and with the encouragement of her coach she was taking the opportunity to grow again.

chapter five

▬

LIGHT YOUR FIRE
WHERE THE SPARKS OF DIVERSITY FLY

My graduate students are all very smart, but they are often very tentative about their goals. They talk to me about their dreams but not how they'll reach them. Some have strong entrepreneurial ideas but struggle to connect with the people who could help make those ideas reality. Others tell me they want a soul mate, yet they can't seem to meet anyone. From the point of view of creativizing, it's really the same challenge. I ask them: Where could you find the sort of people you're looking for? And surprisingly often I hear something like this: I suppose they might belong to this organization, but I don't like to go to those events. Or: My uncle would give me some seed money, but he's kind of hard to deal with. Or: I hear a lot of networking goes on at the coffee shop near the university, but I don't drink coffee.

I tell them: You're not going for the coffee or for the events. Your uncle doesn't have to be your best friend; just be sure you can trust him and that you have a clear understanding of each of your rights and responsibilities, spelled out in a contract. Go where the sparks fly. That's where you have the best chance to light a fire. And sparks fly where things bang up against one another, where there is some collision and some difference—even some conflict. My home state of

Michigan is in a terrible recession, but my city is not—because my city is one of the most diverse in the country. It is mixing creative tension that leads to innovation, yet people are most comfortable with people like themselves. And so they often avoid the uncomfortable, conflict-prone, creative situations where innovation can happen.

Sander, for example, was a programmer with a dream. He wanted to out-Facebook Facebook. And the surprising thing was, he had a shot. He had worked for one of the most innovative computer companies, and he was extremely accomplished when it came to writing computer code. He recognized the potential of social media early on, and he got to work. With a small amount of venture capital, he hired other highly talented technicians to build a social network that was going to be "so much better than Facebook."

After he heard me speak at a technology conference, he started to email me, telling me all about his new product and his plans for it. We were both innovators. Was I interested in becoming a partner? It was clear to me that I couldn't help him. Finally he came to Michigan and waited outside of my office. Then I felt I had to talk to him. He explained to me why his social media network was superior to anything out there. He asked again if I wanted to become his partner.

I said: You've come all this way. Let me give you an accounting of what I see. You don't need me as a partner. You're an innovator, I'm an innovator. Everyone you work with is a technical innovator. You've built this network and it looks technically brilliant, but why would anyone want to use it? Wasn't there anyone on your team who was thinking about that? You've created a flawless social network but without any social appeal. Your trouble is that you haven't surrounded yourself with anyone different from you. You've been refining your technical approach for four years but you have no audience to use what your technicians have built.

What he needed was not more brilliant technical innovations; it was three hundred thousand users who would generate enough money to get his system noticed and bought out by a company that could help him take it to the next level. What he had instead was as appealing as what someone might expect from technical people talking only to other technical people—basically the equivalent of fifteen-year-old boys talking to other fifteen-year-old boys about girls.

But wait, he told me. I don't know those people. I'm not friends with those people. I don't know where to find those people.

Next time around, I told him, start with that. Keep talking to people until you figure out where the sparks of diversity fly.

It's heartbreaking to me how many times I've seen this story play out. Sander's example of the tight little group of the similarly minded and the doomed could be drawn from almost any field where specialization and expertise are essential, but limiting: They could have been musicians, scientists, supporters of a moral or political cause, parents trying to improve their children's school, and so forth. Without a diversity of perspectives and talents, innovations wither and die.

Am I saying you should spend more time with strange people who make you uncomfortable? In a sense, yes. Nationwide, most of us are suffering from an epidemic of just-like-me-ness. Americans have the freedom to move around, and increasingly you find people moving to be near people who look and think just like they do. Cellphones and social networks and other new forms of communication, from this point of view, are a disaster, at least in the way people tend to use them. All they do is make it ever easier to stay connected to people we feel most like, no matter where we are. I see this when I encounter young people abroad: So many of them are on their phones, texting or talking with friends from back home. Even thousands of miles from home, they are stuck in the thought habits of home. Like increasingly stays tied to like, but opposites can't attract if they never get a chance to meet each other.

who can do what you can't?

Part of creativizing is to learn to love—or at least respect—the people and practices that you now hate. As Machiavelli said, "Keep your friends close and your enemies closer." Begin a practice of treating people who approach things from the opposite point of view as your greatest asset. Forget about improving your areas of weakness. Surround yourself, instead, with people who are already good at what you're bad at and work with them. Ask yourself: Who can do what I can't? Who has the skills or the means or the access that I lack? Am I avoiding meeting those people because I'm more comfortable with people like me? Am I afraid to be told there are other ways to do things, other goals that matter? Am I avoiding people who might say I'm doing it all wrong? Try this month to connect with some potentially helpful people who don't make you feel perfectly comfortable. You don't need to set up a formal partnership, at least not yet. For now, focus on expanding your circle so you can discover the powerful diversity of people around you. If you are a parent of a child in public school and you are angry about the state of your school, don't just talk to other angry parents. Talk to some of the teachers and administrators. Talk to the students. If you want to design videogames, don't just talk to other gamers. Talk to people who don't like videogames about what they don't like. Talk to the manager at the local videogame store about what it's like to be in that business.

I'm not saying that every day you need to hear from people who think differently. Sometimes a new idea or a beginning effort needs to be protected from any and all critics for a while, just as some plants have to get started in a pot indoors before they're strong enough to be transferred to a garden. But as soon as you feel you can tolerate it, start seeking these people out—not people who will tear you down but people who will spot approaches you've missed.

chapter six

─────

THE CAVALRY ISN'T COMING

I fly a hundred thousand miles or more each year, and usually when I get off my plane I'm met by the driver of a black car. I've probably talked with hundreds of drivers doing the same job, chauffeuring people like me around and hustling for tips. In St. Louis, my client regularly hired the same young guy to meet my plane. He liked to talk to me about his work. No one told him to do that, he just started talking. In one conversation I asked him: Who do you work for? He said all of his business was with two companies. I asked: Do they know you? What's your specialty? He said other car services required a half day's notice, but he would come if they called at the last minute. Also, he was willing to drive long-distance: If they needed a ride from St. Louis to Chicago, he'd get on the highway.

I said: If you're valuable to them, if you've got a special niche, one of those companies might be willing to commit to a long-term arrangement with you, so they know they can always get a ride from you when they want it. And if they're willing to make a formal arrangement, you could probably find a business partner who would put up some money to buy some cars.

This advice wasn't special. I've given it to other drivers and equivalent advice to lots of other solo practitioners in different businesses over the years. But the next time I saw this young man, he said, "I want to tell you something. I'm no longer just a driver. I got a partner and we bought two Lincolns. I own the company." He wasn't rich, but the whole way he talked about his life had changed: *I own the company.*

Psychologists call this self-authorizing behavior. This young man changed his behavior and made himself the author of his own life. No one had told him to talk to me while he drove me to my conference. No one had told him to act on what I said. No one told him how to seek out someone in his community who could put up money to buy two cars. But he saw that his life—and almost everyone's life—is like that moment in the old Western when a townsperson rides back into town with the bad news: "We're on our own. The cavalry isn't coming." To me, that moment in the movie, when a man rides in, dusty, exhausted, and grim, shows the key existential moment in creativizing. It's the moment that you realize no one else is going to save you. You're bankrupt and no one is going to bail you out; your marriage is broken and it's not going to get fixed; you've got an illness and it can't be wished away; you have the same unrealized dream you've always had, and no one but you can make it come true. The feeling at the moment is hard to take, but it clears your vision. Now you see what the townspeople in the Western see: If we're going to get rescued, we'll have to rescue ourselves.

Of course, we all try to put that moment off. We deny. We criticize. We blame. Everyone does it—people come to me all the time with stories of the outrageous bad luck they've had, the unfairness and stupidity of the people they had to work with, the outrages committed by the evildoers who've done them wrong. Some martial vast evidence to prove the thesis that life sucks. It's like what you hear on political talk shows, at either end of the spectrum: The other side is not just wrong, they are crazy, immoral, and evil—probably all three. Even if these views are sometimes correct, they aren't any help if what you want is to creativize. Because that kind of thinking comes from a position of reaction, of criticism. People talking that way are not self-authorizing; they're just criticizing, saying everything that's wrong with what others do but nothing about what would work better. Innovation can't be done by critics. It takes authors.

When I hear people stuck in the reactionary mode, people who are too busy critiquing and explaining and blaming to self-authorize and start building something new, I ask them: Okay, well, what would *you* do? Let's say you're right and people around you are crazy. What would a sane person do? Let's say this or that member of Congress is an idiot. How would you solve the problem? Forget your vicious boss for a moment, your undermining parents. What would a good boss say? What would good parents do? These questions shift your thinking because they stop you from endlessly moving away from something and start you moving toward something new—that is, they start you innovating.

rescue yourself

I saw this pattern with Kate, who always said she wanted to find a spiritual community but never seemed to find it. Kate's family was Jewish. She grew up going to synagogue and even taught Hebrew school as a teenager. As she got older, though, she left a lot of her childhood connections to religion behind. After college, she moved to a big city and became very busy with her career. Religious observance dropped out of her life except for once or twice a year when she went home and attended her family's synagogue. Years passed, Kate married and had children, and now she was even busier. But she found that she missed being involved in a synagogue and in the community it provided when she was younger. She told me she wanted to make room for a more spiritual life, especially now that she had kids. Her husband seemed willing to go along, but not to be a leader in this area. So from time to time, Kate visited one of the synagogues in the vicinity.

With each visit, almost as soon as she walked in, she would feel put off because it wasn't what she expected. One synagogue had a young, very casual rabbi who played acoustic guitar and said too few of the traditional prayers in Hebrew for Kate's taste. Another was more traditional but required the men and women to sit in separate parts of the sanctuary, which did not suit her. Years continued to go by, and as Kate's kids got older she kept telling me that this year was the year she would find a synagogue, but every time she tried one, she ruled it out. Then inevitably she would get busy again and more time would go by.

Kate was stuck in the reactionary mode. She was evaluating and criticizing, not creating. She reminded me of certain older, unmarried people I've known who decide later in life that they want a spouse after all. They are experts at going on dates and evaluating what's wrong with every possible candidate. And they're right—there's something wrong with everyone. We're human. But we're worthwhile anyway. People don't marry when they've found perfection because there is no perfection. They marry when they've found someone they love whose faults they can accept, and who can accept their faults in return.

I told Kate that if she wanted to find a spiritual home for her family, she had to go on more visits. If she'd try all main options in a short period of time, one or two would look good compared to the rest. But most important, she had to go on those visits with a different mindset. She had to walk in and ask herself: What would I do if this was my synagogue? How would I find a place for myself here? How would I find a place for my family? She couldn't expect that someone else was going to set up everything perfectly for her. The cavalry wasn't coming. No matter which synagogue her family joined, she would need to roll up her sleeves and innovate a way they could find what they needed at that imperfect place. She was going to have to rescue herself.

become self-authorizing

As you think through your innovation goals, notice your feelings. Are you feeling helpless or impatient? Are you waiting for the cavalry to come charging to the rescue? Well, I'm sorry. The cavalry isn't coming. Do you feel stagnant or stuck? Is there always a criticism on the tip of your tongue? These are signs that you aren't self-authorizing. Instead, try this:

- Picture what you want.
- See it clearly.
- Now picture someone who could advise you about taking a possible next step, someone who could help you answer the question: What could *I* do to make this work?

Find that person. Have a conversation. Don't criticize their ideas, just collect possibilities, imagine how the story could go if it had a happy ending. Be an author, not a critic. Then try one of that person's suggestions or one of your own ideas. Without anyone telling you to, do an experiment in your own life. Start a new chapter. Move your story forward.

chapter seven

RIDE WHAT MOVES

Fiona always felt pulled in two different career directions. In college, she took business classes but also studio art classes—drawing and painting especially. After graduation, she accepted a job with a bank, and continued to work for banks for years, developing a particular expertise in online services. At the same time, she continued to sketch and paint on weekends. She took vacations that let her trace the steps of the painters she admired most. She went to the galleries in her area. Yet over time, she felt increasingly left out of the creative life she had enjoyed in her student days.

She was especially discouraged by the small number of people who saw her work and the wall she hit whenever she tried to find representation with an art gallery. Where she lived, the number of galleries was shrinking, and it seemed as if they only showed the work of art school graduates or of artists who had successful contemporary artists as their champions. It appeared to Fiona to be a closed world, yet she knew she could never take years off to attend art school just to break in.

Meanwhile she continued to have success developing online banking offerings for smaller banks. Regional banks were now able to reach customers all over the country, and this realization gave her the idea to look for online opportunities for visual artists. In time she found an online graphic arts group that shared their work on the Web and marketed to a far wider audience than they could reach through any local gallery. Unlike the local art scene where Fiona lived, the online arts community was growing quickly and was more open to outsiders. Fiona began showing and even selling her work online. Through these new connections, she was invited to participate in some traditional group gallery shows in other cities, galleries that used the Internet to build publicity. The skills that had made her a success in her banking career were helping to make her a successful working artist as well.

Fiona succeeded in the same way as my friend at Reuters who traveled around India and saw that although laptops were scarce among farmers and small businesspeople, cellphones were booming. He asked himself: If I want to sell commodities information, and they only have cellphones, can cellphones take me where I want to go? He made the most of the technology that was "moving." Similarly, Fiona realized that she had already mastered a multimedia technology that was on the move and that could help her get to where she wanted to go.

Everything around us is either growing or dying—that may sound harsh, but it's simply how it is. Successful innovation requires us to notice what is moving and growing around us, and to find ways to harness its energy to get us where we want to go. Newton's First Law states that an object in motion tends to stay in motion, whereas an object at rest tends to stay at rest. If you can climb onto something that is already in motion, it will save you a great deal of energy, compared to pushing that thing yourself. Along the same lines, there is an economic principal called "value migration," which states that as conditions change, the first to recognize them, and to invest in or capitalize on these shifts, stands to make the greatest amount of profit. Some of the "accidental billionaires" who rode Facebook to their fortunes, as portrayed in the movie *The Social Network*, provided only a small amount of cash or some early networking, but because they were the first to ride this new phenomenon that was moving, they saw huge benefits.

The choice to ride what moves can make the difference between innovation and slow decay for an individual, an organization, even a city or country. Consider Kalamazoo, Michigan. Located halfway between Chicago and Detroit, Kalamazoo was crowned the "All-American City" by *Life* magazine in the 1960s. It was home to postwar corporate giants like Fisher Body, Checker Motors, the Upjohn Company, and that symbol of the generation in motion, Gibson Guitars. Frank Lloyd Wright created some of his greatest architectural marvels here and nestled them in between the painted ladies that housed the local gentry. The city even closed its main thoroughfare to create a little European flair downtown—the first outdoor pedestrian shopping mall in the country. Kalamazoo was an emblem of forward-thinking and self-reliant success.

But slowly things unraveled. Manufacturing left the snowbelt for warmer lands, as did the city's creative and enterprising youth. Roads cracked, factories failed. For three decades the city was mentioned as yet another example of Northern Blight, if it was mentioned as anything besides a town with a funny name.

And then it happened. A group of anonymous donors got together and raised an enormous trust to fund the college education of every child that graduated from a Kalamazoo public school. They called it the Kalamazoo Promise. Families that owned homes in the school district began sending their children to state of Michigan universities and community colleges for free. People began to move to Kalamazoo for the sake of their children. Neighborhoods were rehabilitated. The momentum that had shifted from good to bad now shifted back toward good again. Like the unexpected hit in a baseball game that starts a rally and wins the game, which starts a winning streak that ends with a pennant, Kalamazoo was moving again, and innovators came to ride. Beauty shops and coffee joints popped up alongside Internet developers and art studios. Businesses began to give the old town a fresh look as biotech and material science firms started springing up. Medical device firms expanded in the area and big pharmaceutical companies came with them, bringing good jobs. Even one of the city's own, Derek Jeter, became the captain of the lauded New York Yankees baseball team. Kalamazoo was back, and what had gotten it started was an energizing act—aimed at improving one isolated issue—that set things in motion.

That's why I say: No matter what in your life you are trying to innovate, look to ride what moves. Just as I suggested that you make time to notice bad weather coming, I encourage you to make time to notice the areas of growth and fresh opportunity. Get to know them. Talk to people making use of them. They may not have any obvious connection to what you want to do. They may be as different as oil painting and online marketplaces. Still, find chances to experiment with them. The transition to the area that moves won't be seamless—you can't expect to notice an area of growth and then immediately see how it can take you where you want to go. For now, as you establish the habits of creativizing, it's enough to get to know what's on the move.

make sure what moves is going your way

I want to end this chapter with a couple of caveats. First, I'm not trying to say that this process is seamless. I was reminded of this when I started to use Twitter. When I heard about it, I wasn't sure I liked it or that I was any good at it. But I was sure that it was something on the move. So I started to tweet, even as I felt uncomfortable.

I got some advice from marketing experts. They said the goal was to develop as big an audience as I could, so I could send that audience "a highly specific brand image" of me as "the Dean of Innovation," as often as possible. But I didn't want to hammer home a message; I wanted to talk to those people who are thinking about the things that interest me—my people, who are on same road. I wanted to share what was on my mind as I continued to explore innovation—to make it more like a salon or a good conversation at the counter of the coffee shop.

Then I met a twenty-one-year-old undergraduate who tweets all the time. I told him what I wanted to do and he said yes, that's the way I do it. I find things others have written that I think are interesting to the community I want to reach. Then I message people to ask what they think. That way I can have a more robust conversation—I'm not just blasting everyone with a marketing message.

I asked this young man to work with me for a semester, to teach me to translate my thoughts into the formal language of Twitter and to help me find the community that wants to have the kind of meaningful conversation I want to have. We agreed that once a week we'd sit down together and he'd be my Twitter coach. I knew it would take time. But I also felt reassured: I had found someone who could help me with the slow process of learning to ride what moves.

At the same time, I want to be clear that riding what moves does not mean jumping on every bandwagon that comes along. For example, by the time this book comes out, some of the examples mentioned in its pages will be more than familiar—everyone who is listening will know that healthcare is a booming field or that Twitter replaced some earlier forms of media. These things that were once new and unusually rich opportunities become ordinary parts of the landscape. If you want to know what's going to be next, what is getting into motion today and creating the opportunity to ride, you'll need to keep watching the weather.

chapter eight

EFFICIENCY CAN KILL YOU—
THE 20–80 RULE

Often, I've noticed, when I talk to someone about the need to innovate, that person will respond by telling me how much he or she is doing already. I think of Jon, a manager who worked for a corporate client of mine. I was helping his company develop new approaches to efficiency, but he wasn't using any of them. He wasn't even giving them a try. In fact, he was running his team exactly the way he had run it three years earlier.

When I asked Jon if he had considered trying some of the company's new initiatives with his team, he turned his computer screen around so I could see it and brought up his work schedule. "Look at this calendar!" he cried. "I'm working seventy-hour weeks. You won't find a more efficient employee in this entire company!"

I didn't disagree. He was working very long hours and his scheduling was highly efficient. I admired his drive and his focus, and I told him so. But I also told him that from the point of view of innovation, his efficiency was not a plus. It was evidence that he was getting it wrong.

These days we make productivity something like a religion. We believe that if we are productive enough, organized enough, task-focused enough, this will save us from the fact that our lives are overcommitted. Mega-bestsellers like *Getting Things Done: The Art of Stress-Free Productivity* by David Allen and *The Seven Habits of Highly Effective People: Powerful Lessons in Personal Change* by Stephen R. Covey, have taken rules originally designed to make large operations such as factories and hospitals more efficient, and applied those rules to our personal lives. Perhaps the most important of these rules is the 80–20 rule, also known as the Pareto principle. It states that 80 percent of the results we're trying to achieve come from only 20 percent of the causes. It was first inspired by the observation that 80 percent of the peas in someone's garden came from 20 percent of the pods, and it's been found to hold for many other examples of productivity: 80 percent of a company's income tends to come from 20 percent of the customers. Most of the distractions and wasted time in your life tend to be created by a small number of distracting, wasteful people. So today, many of us focus on trying to do more for the most important clients or customers and to avoid whoever is wasteful or doesn't show results.

In our personal lives as well, many of us try to use our time where it's more productive, where we can see immediate results. Now we carry portable electronics so we can fit ten more computer activities into our day while we're carpooling kids to activities; we carry smartphones so that even when we're walking the dog, or sleeping, we can be "on call" and available to move projects forward for those extra-valuable 20 percent of the clients, or those extra-important people in our lives. That can be a good thing, but the trouble is, if you constantly optimize your life for productivity, it doesn't give you more time. It uses up more of your time. You become like Jon the manager, with an ever-longer, ever-more-tightly-packed schedule. As useful as these approaches can be, our quest for productivity can cost us our capacity to innovate.

Like Jon, we complete many tasks but we wind up too busy to try anything new. Instead of improving our lives, we just do more and more of the same old tasks in the same old ways. Even if your goal is short-term results, you may not have time to notice that conditions have changed, and the parts of your life or your work that used to pay off the best no longer do—there is still a most valuable 20 percent, but it's a different 20 percent than it was before, and you don't have time to learn how it's changed.

forget the 80–20 rule

My colleague Robert Quinn describes this as "breaking the logic of task pursuit." To make time for improvements, we need to forget the 80–20 rule. Innovation requires us to experiment, to follow new paths even though some—many—will be wrong turns or dead ends. But that doesn't mean you need to stop your life and do nothing but experiment and explore. That would be very difficult, and it often backfires: I've known too many people who have quit a job to get to work on their dream, only to run out of funds and retreat to another job no better than the first.

Instead of trying to innovate 100 percent of your life at once, pick a narrow part of your life and concentrate on innovating that 20 percent. It's much easier to make big changes in a small area of life than it is to make even moderate changes all across your life. If you want to become a musician and you've never played before, which would you rather do, commit to practice for an hour every day, or to practice all day every Saturday?

I call this the 20–80 rule. It is easier to change 20 percent of a company or a life by 80 percent than it is to change 80 percent of that company or that life by even 20 percent. Innovation requires us to break off and protect a relatively small piece of time and then, in that protected area, forget efficiency and short-term gains in favor of experimentation and long-term improvements. This is what Teri the schoolteacher did when she found part-time teaching work and used the rest of her time for baking and building up her knowledge and connections with potential customers. Eighty percent of her life was producing income in the old way, by teaching, but 20 percent was innovating a new career, baking. This approach is also what I've been asking you to do here in Step I: Make time to learn and practice these new approaches, even scheduling in time to watch the weather, for example, despite the fact that you won't see results for a while.

PRACTICE THE 20–80 RULE
- Set aside scheduled time to creativize.
- Protect that creative time as if it were as valuable to you as your most productive hours.
- Accept that you won't see short-term results. Your goal in that narrow, protected piece of time is to work toward the innovations that will improve your life for the future, not for today. Over time, like plants, these small growths that don't seem good for anything will mature and bear fruit.
- Combine the 20–80 rule with "We grow when our life sucks or when we're on a roll."

Am I saying that striving for efficiency is always a mistake? That those mega-bestsellers have everything all wrong? No. There is a time in the cycle of innovation for narrowing your options and trying to be as efficient as you can. Later in this book, we will see how essential it is to shift back and forth between the 20–80 rule and the 80–20 rule. But that time is not at the beginning of the cycle, when you creativize.

step II

REVISE YOUR APPROACH
WITH PRISMATIC THINKING

If you do not change direction,
you may end up where you are heading.
—Lao-tzu

Imagine that a meteor is hurtling toward Earth, as in a science fiction movie. You are the U.S. president and you have a month to innovate a solution or life as we know it will end. There is no one who has solved this problem before. Who would you put in charge? Would it be someone who says, "I don't know a lot about outer space, but I'm very careful and organized, so let's move very carefully. I'll study the problem for three weeks, and then build one solution that looks on paper like it will work and fire it at five minutes to midnight"?

I hope not. Careful research and planning are valuable, but in a fishing trip as unusual as this one, you don't have any idea where the fish will be biting or what it will take to reel them in. You'd do much better to call a hundred people with different kinds of expertise about meteors, physics, space travel, explosives, videogames—any aspect of the problem that seemed in any way relevant. Give them twenty billion dollars and tell them to start making lots of prototypes. As you observe the work of those hundred, you might pick six conventional scientists and six wild-eyed pistol-wavers and ask them all to build their best attempts. Deflecting the meteor might well take several of those attempts. In fact, I have a strong sense of what is likely to happen. Most or all of the conventional approaches are likely to fail. Some of the moderately inventive approaches might slow the meteor down a little. Most of the weird ideas from left field will go nowhere, but one of them will finally knock the meteor out of the sky.

How do I know? Because when you have a problem that new, it's like fishing for giant squid: They've barely ever been seen because they live so deep. They can't be studied because no one knows where to find them, and so you have to go outside your fixed ideas of good fishing and try a lot of new alternatives. The point is not that traditional expertise and careful planning are not valuable, but that they are not the *most* valuable approach in this kind of situation.

In a science-fiction disaster scenario like this one, it's fairly obvious that quickly trying a lot of different solutions is going to serve you better than slowly preparing one safe and familiar attempt. But in more realistic scenarios, it can be harder to see how our approach matters. Whether in our home life or work life, too often we don't even consider the full range of approaches that are open to us, with the result that the best approach is often excluded at the start. The results can be disastrous.

When the Deepwater Horizon oil drilling platform blew up in the Gulf of Mexico, a spokesperson for British Petroleum came on television, expressed his condolences to the families of the workers, and offered this appraisal of the situation: The damaged well is a mile down, and we believe we know what went wrong and how much oil is being released from the well. Hearing that, I suspected right away that this was going to be trouble and that oil was going to keep pouring into the Gulf for some time. First of all, this accident was diagnosed as if it were a standard problem, one the company was familiar with, not something new and unique. But this was a new type of problem that required unbridled invention. This was a meteor hurtling from space.

When interviewed by the press, the person in charge of the operation was quick to say that the situation was under control. He was what I call a "Control" innovator, used to a situation that's established and well known. When he innovates, he adds value by making minor improvements and keeping tight control. Companies that are big, complex, and successful know how to make things work and keep them running smoothly with small improvements applied on a giant scale. They avoid trying anything radically different because that could put all they have built at risk. So he was protecting his reputation and that of his company, to prevent them from being seen to fail in public.

I should make clear that I'm not criticizing him personally or suggesting that he was not suited to his regular position. In this highly unusual situation, however, a different type of leader may have been better suited to developing breakthrough solutions. To use a sports analogy: They didn't make the player substitution when it was called for. They needed someone who could take an entirely different approach, someone who understood that when you have a serious problem or a challenge and you don't have a lot of information, you have to hedge—just like in portfolio investment—not just to spread the risk but to fish for the upside opportunity: When you don't know where the fish are biting or what they're eating today, you need to fish a lot of different spots on the river with a lot of different lures. It's a far messier approach and there will be many small failures, but it's a much more valuable approach to this type of challenge because it gives you the best chance, by the end of the day, of catching the unusual fish you're after. The second step in the process of innovating you is to revise your approach. In this second part of the book, I'll show that there is always more than one potentially valuable approach to innovation. In fact, there are four, though blending is possible. I'll help you learn to see the full range, so you can pick the one most valuable for reaching your goals in the situation you're in now, not the situation you were in yesterday or the one that's most familiar and comfortable.

chapter nine

THINK AROUND THE COLORS

To start, let's consider Caroline. A real estate broker with an ailing father, she met with her accountant at tax time and came to a realization even bigger than her tax bill: In the past year, she'd spent nearly twice what she'd earned, mostly due to her father's increasing home healthcare costs. Her savings and credit had sustained her for the short run, but now a meteor of debt was hurtling toward her life, threatening her mortgage, her car loan, her vacation next summer, as well as what concerned her most, her ability to care for her father.

Caroline was normally a careful person, and her work life was characterized by responsibility and frugal use of resources. Her real estate clients appreciated the detailed checklists she prepared for herself and for them, and the many small touches with which she helped each client prepare a house to go on the market. In dealing with the costs of her father's illness, she had taken the approach that was most comfortable to her: She cut back on her own spending on things like restaurants and new clothes, and took time away from work to care for him (reducing her costs for hired home healthcare workers). Yet as she sat with her accountant, she realized that her usual approach wasn't going to solve the problem. Many of her father's expenses could not be trimmed any further, and she was already spending money she had hoped to put toward retirement.

Seeing that her habitual approach was failing, Caroline asked her accountant to help her decide what to do. He made it sound frustratingly simple. The problem, he said, was that she was spending more than she was earning. She could spend less, and perform more of her father's care herself—this was what she had tried already, and so far it wasn't working. Alternatively, she could make more money, either at her current job or some other job. ("Easy for him to say," Caroline thought.) Or she could get help from family or friends. As he walked her to the door, her accountant told her, "One way or another, you've got to get your income in line with your expenses."

Caroline knew that already. She also knew, already, that she needed a new approach. The situation made her miserable—she was in a rut and she was ready to try something new. But given her changed situation, given who she was, what was the best approach?

This was a job for what I call "prismatic thinking," a method for finding your own best approach for whatever kind of innovation you want. No matter who you are or what you are trying to innovate, there are only four basic approaches to innovation. Almost everyone has one approach that he or she unconsciously prefers, just as almost everyone is naturally left-handed or right-handed. For many people, their approach seems so "natural" that they may never have even put into words what it is. So the first step in prismatic thinking is to identify the approach you have generally taken up until now. Once you do that, you can learn to craft an approach that suits your current goals, blending the most useful parts of all four approaches to get you where you need to go.

learn the colors

Here's what Caroline's accountant got right: Somehow, she needed to get her expenses and her income in line while meeting her obligations to herself and her father. He also got right that there were only four basic ways to do that. When Caroline came to me, we took it further. It's not just that there were four basic ways Caroline could get her finances in order, but there are only four main approaches to innovation of every kind: You can create, compete, collaborate, or control. In all my work, those are the categories of approaches that I see time and again with businesses and with individuals as well. I find it easiest to explain and to teach this central concept by assigning a color to each of the four approaches. Why colors? Think of a prism. Light is everywhere, but unless the power goes out, we take it for granted. Only when we see a rainbow or when someone shines light through a prism are we reminded that the light we live and work by every day contains all the colors of the rainbow. In the same way, every challenge or problem can draw on all the "colors" of innovation, but most of the time we're not even aware that those colors are all around us. In prismatic thinking, we break the light of innovation into its component colors. Each of these is a way to make your situation new and improved, yet each one gets different results. I describe them this way:

• COLLABORATE. Caroline could team up with others, move in with a friend, or advertise for a housemate to defray the cost of her mortgage. She could take a nursing class so she could provide more care for her father by herself. With effort and care, she might encourage other family members, who lived far away, to find ways of helping care for her father. She might make an arrangement to share her car with someone who needed it when it was not essential for her, for example, on weekends. If she could find others to collaborate with her, she could change her situation for the better—and the results would look different from any of the other approaches. *In the Competing Values mode, this is the* Collaborate *or yellow approach.*

• CREATE. Caroline could take an entirely new approach. While sitting with her accountant, she found herself thinking about all the people she knew who were facing similarly confusing life situations—

financial challenges, aging parents with increasing needs, doubts about their plans for the future. She found herself daydreaming: What if she and her accountant together launched a business that would offer people help in meeting the full range of their challenges, both financial and personal? Might that new business provide a new source of income while helping her deal with her own crisis? Maybe, she thought, if she got creative enough, she could find a way to turn this whole mess into a new career. *In my model, this is the* Create *or green approach.*

 • COMPETE. Caroline could earn more, succeed bigger, leave spending pretty much alone, and focus on increasing revenue. She could commit more time and resources to profitable work and become more competitive in her field. She could hit her targets and get a bonus. If she could earn enough money, her high levels of spending for her father and herself would no longer be a problem. They would be fine just as they were. If she could become more competitive as an earner, that would change her situation, too—though her situation would be new and improved in a very different way than if she focused on cutting back and becoming more efficient. *In my model this is the* Compete *or blue approach.*

 • CONTROL. Caroline could cut expenses even further, become more efficient, and waste less. She could handle more of her father's care personally. If Caroline could do more with less, she could cut her spending until it matched her current income. Exploring this approach, she considered bigger changes than ever before: moving from a house to an apartment, giving up her lease on a luxury car and instead leasing a less expensive, used model, and so forth. By controlling waste and increasing her efficiency, she might be able to make ends meet. *In my innovation framework, this is the* Control *or red approach.*

I want to be clear that I'm not saying there are four approaches and Create (green) is the innovative one. I'm saying that all four approaches can be powerful ways to create innovation, but in different ways.

Every person—like every business, every community, and even every country—favors one of these four approaches over the others. You may already have a sense of which approach describes you. You may also be feeling, already, that none of these can describe you completely. Both of these responses are essential for rethinking your approach to innovation. Just as almost every person is either right-handed or left-handed, and favors the dominant hand when doing manual tasks, you need to know which you are and when that might not be an advantage. At the same time, just because you are left-handed doesn't mean you'd agree to tie your right hand behind your back. In reality, all situations, practices, and people employ multiple approaches to innovation, but they tend to favor one over the others, for better or worse, depending on the goal. The question is how best to use your hands, or your approaches to innovation, together.

To begin revising your approach to innovation, I want to make sure you know which of the four basic approaches comes most naturally to you, what it's good for, and where you might encounter its limits. I will start by giving "portraits" of the categories. As you read them, consider which one sounds most like you, but also what resemblances you may see in the other three portraits.

If you feel you would prefer a more formal assessment of your characteristic approach to innovation, you can turn to the assessment in the Appendix at the back of this book, or visit the InnovationYou.com website. There you will find a free online assessment tool. Comparable to the existing "Competing Values" business version, which has been taken by thirty-eight thousand professionals worldwide, this quiz will clearly show you which "hand" you favor.

innovation you model

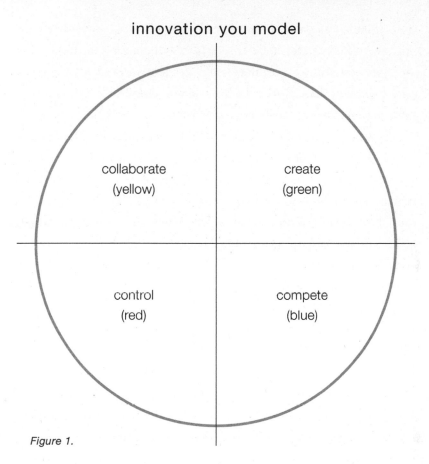

Figure 1.

collaborate (yellow)

Collaborates—or yellows—connect. They like to work where they can nurture a community based on trust, commitment, and lasting relationships—the sorts of places that get known as "great places to work." If they had a motto, it might be, "Let's do this together—and make it last." Parents who tend toward the Collaborate perspective, for instance, emphasize school as a place for lifelong learning, networking, and friendship. With or without children, many work in schools and universities, in human resource departments, and in the helping professions. In a business, yellows extend their commitment to community beyond fellow colleagues to include customers, whom they often see as partners in the business. Think about how Singapore Air differentiates itself through its outstanding customer service, or how Linux has developed its software so that anyone associated with its community can use it and add to it. Many Internet start-ups take a Collaborate approach.

Because the Collaborate approach is identified with family and clan and work for the greater good, the approach may be interpreted as spiritual: It appears as identification and commitment to a particular set of mores and beliefs. We see the Collaborate approach in the life of Mother Teresa. She was compelled to create something larger than an organization, nationality, or religion. Mother Teresa created a movement built on values, compassion, and service to bring dignity and mercy to the sick and poor of all faiths. The Collaborate force is typically associated with the slowest forms of growth because it focuses on building the underlying organizational culture and competencies required to sustain it.

Taken too far, however, a Collaborate approach becomes a pleasure cruise where everyone helps everyone else feel all right, but no one gets anywhere. Think of an elementary school that emphasizes self-esteem so much that it excludes practical skills—the kind of school where the kids are happy, everyone scores high on self-esteem, but nobody is learning to read.

create (green)

As you might expect from the term, Creates (greens) experiment and explore. Generalists and artists, they enjoy finding multiple answers to problems and are able to easily shift directions while they are problem solving. The Create profile describes the kind of people most of us think of first when we think of creativity or innovation: the scientist in his lab, the novelist in his garret, the musician playing all night in a club, the computer engineer inventing the new software or device that will change the way all of us live.

Creates live to generate new ideas and approaches, and they guard their freedom. They will set aside norms and rules in the service of their emerging vision, which usually emphasizes new ideas, flexibility, and adaptability. Their motto could be, "Let's try this another way." In companies, Creates develop new products, methods, and services that can change the entire landscape of an industry. Walt Disney, who invented so many kinds of entertainment we had never seen before, was certainly a Create type.

Innovations that come as a result of a Create approach can be the biggest and most valuable forms of change: new discoveries, original processes or points of view, unique expressions of vision. People with this tendency have the potential to change the world around them by creating entirely new categories. But while Create innovations can have the biggest impact when they succeed, they are also the slowest to develop, and they have the greatest chance of failure. (Even the most successful are like Babe Ruth: The home run king was also the leader in strikeouts.) Taken too far, a Create approach can become chaotic, an endless series of wild experiments with no useful results.

compete (blue)

Competes (blues) love a challenge. Blues see the world as a game with winners and losers, and feel motivated to innovate by clear goals and specific rewards: money, power, fame, and other tangible forms of success. These are people who like to get things done and see the results. They find competition exhilarating and enjoy the hard work necessary to win. If Competes had a motto, it might be the Nike slogan, "Just do it." Parents who tend to the Compete perspective emphasize that school is a place to earn high grades and win access to profitable careers. In a company, you often find this type of innovator in the finance or marketing department. This form of innovation is the fastest of all four to show results, and it can achieve prosperity and physical fitness for the people who use it best. Thomas Edison is remembered as an inventor, but his genius was, I think, in his Compete nature: He was goal-oriented and chose talent in his labs the way George Steinbrenner chose it for the New York Yankees. Everyone outside New York hates the Yankees because they're so damn good. Love them or hate them, it must be acknowledged that they pick winners and then pay what it takes to keep them around.

Taken too far, however, the Compete approach can lead to reckless pursuit of short-term gain at the expense of anything else: "Winning isn't everything, it's the only thing." It is also hard to sustain: its "sweatshop" approach gives little concern to long-term well-being.

control (red)

Controls (reds) are systematic. Careful and practical, they innovate in the opposite way from greens. Rather than trying to invent a game-changing new creation, reds build change in small, careful steps by taking something that is already good and modifying it to make it better. The Control approach, more than the other three, is focused not only on improving growth but on reducing failures to ensure security and efficiency. Henry Ford was a red innovator: He invented nothing, but he perfected everything, making the complex new system of the assembly line work to produce cars that ordinary working people could afford. In the Control worldview, there is a right way and a wrong way, governed by fixed laws. A meter always contains one hundred centimeters. Highborn ladies never wear white after Labor Day. Interpretations are of little significance in the face of rules and standards. Data wins the day. This approach is closely associated with technology, systems, and engineering employed to streamline complexity and increase efficiency and quality. Firms like Toyota and Dell are Control innovators, taking products that their competitors already make—cars, computers—and adding their own small innovations, strictly enforced. The results are often both higher in quality and less expensive than what came before.

You find reds in engineering departments or in situations where a complex and potentially dangerous system must run properly— nuclear power plants, surgical theaters, airplanes and space ships manufacturers, and the armed forces. They expect their rank to be respected and their rules to be followed. If they had a motto, it might be, "Make it work better." Ray Kroc, who bought a little restaurant chain called McDonald's and systematically reproduced identical restaurants around the world, was a Control, a red.

The Control approach is the least risky and the most reliable, but its benefits are the smallest. Taken too far, it becomes a tangle of rules, red tape, and bureaucracy that can strangle the very creativity it requires.

understand your approach

Many people I have worked with, in the context of innovating both in business and for personal benefit, come to recognize themselves primarily in one portrait: "I'm a yellow" or "I'm a blue." Others have one area in which they work most naturally and a different area that describes the goals that motivate and inspire them. To use me as an example, I'm clearly a green—the way I innovate most comfortably is to create. I experiment, I try for new solutions, I'm willing to take big risks and wait a long time in order to come up with a game-changing solution. But I'm not a typical Create type—you won't find me in an artist's studio or a science lab. I'll be over at the business school or in my business innovation lab. What comes naturally to me is creativity, but creativity in the service of helping my clients and my students to compete and win. With me, it's never art for art's sake. In other words, I'm a green, for sure, but I'm the bluest green you've ever met.

Try describing your innovation style now, either as a single color or in terms of two: I'm a _____. Or, I'm a _____, but I'm a very _____ _____.

How can you be sure? Here are some clues to your innovation nature.

how do you react to a crisis?

Imagine you have to take responsibility for a five-year-old for an afternoon—your child, your grandchild, the child of a family member or a friend; for this little exercise it doesn't matter. You take him to a nearby playground. Although you think you are paying close attention, you look up and he is at the top of a small climbing structure, losing his balance, falling to the ground. What comes out of your mouth as he starts to wail and you rush to his side?

- A Collaborate type, a yellow, might cry, "It's okay! I'm here with you. I'm right here," emphasizing connection.
- A Create, a green, might say, "What happened? What were you doing?" And then lead the child to reconstruct his movements and think about other ways to climb more safely next time.
- A Compete, a blue, might say, "Oh, that hurt, didn't it?" Meaning: That's a loser move, so remember for the future.
- A Control, a red, is likely to say, "Don't do that! That's dangerous!"

In a crisis, we tend to fall back on our dominant or most comfortable (and comforting) mode of fixing a problem. It's true of more serious events as well. Consider the death of someone you cared about. How did you respond?

- Collaborates generally need to connect with people, so they will surround themselves with others, for example, by talking to everyone they meet at the hospital or the funeral home.

- Creates, by contrast, do a lot of creative thinking. They may observe the situation around them with an artist's eye, make notes, and write or tell stories. (Joan Didion's bestselling memoir about deaths in her family, *The Year of Magical Thinking*, is an example of a Create falling back on her natural strengths in the face of adversity and grief.)
- Competes will find themselves a challenge to overcome, for example, by driving everyone else where they need to go, making all of the logistical arrangements, or negotiating hard about a medical bill. They set themselves tasks they can try to beat.
- Controls will take control of the situation by doing what they feel is correct and proper, perhaps by going to church every day and continuing to do exactly what they've always done because that's what the person who is ailing or deceased would want.

In all of these ways, people tend to innovate a role for themselves in a personal crisis by collapsing back to what they are—to what's most deeply grounding for them. Consider your own first impulse in a similar situation and what that tells you about your natural "color."

notice who pushes your buttons

If we want to know what we really are, we can look to whoever makes us extremely uncomfortable. For example, I was in a meeting recently with a CEO who was correct in what he was saying, but he was mean. Everything he said came out harder and more critical than it needed to be. I drove home angry, and finally I asked myself: Why does this guy bug me so much? I had to admit it was because I can be like that. He was a blue and was hypercompetitive, not at all concerned about the hurt he might inflict as he showed others in his company why he had the best ideas for moving the company forward. I thought: That could be me, but I don't want to be that way. After that, I tried to be more aware of tempering the destructive emotional aspects of the Compete approach.

When someone really gets under your skin, ask yourself, honestly, what is so disturbing about that person. It might be that the person is the opposite of you and behaves in the way you most want to avoid. Or it might be that this person is like you and demonstrates for the entire world to see the attributes you least like about yourself.

what gives you energy and what drains it?

My work requires that I travel a whole lot. Sometimes, coming back from the other side of the world at the end of a long trip when I may not have really slept for the past forty-eight hours, all I want to do is collapse. But if I get on the phone with someone who has a great innovation story or a really interesting case study of a business that needs to be turned around, it doesn't matter how tired I am. The energy comes back. I can talk about those topics all day. That shows me that I am truly a green, and in particular a very blue sort of green, because those are the areas that restore me. What about you? Are there topics, problems or challenges that seem to refresh you, even though they take work?

where do you soar?

I've always loved to perform, and in a sense performance, the theatrical aspect of my work, has seemed to love me back. If I know I have to give a speech, I don't have to do a lot of preparation. I've made many mistakes in various aspects of my career, but I always get a good response to performances and presentations. I get excited but I don't suffer with nervousness the way many do before public speaking. Being onstage and improvising is a ball I know I can hit, an aspect of my life where I can soar. Theatrical performance is of course an art, a green area. I know I'm a green in part because when I'm innovating in green ways I feel yeah, sure: *I can do this.* So consider the areas where you soar. Make sure you distinguish between soaring and just being optimistic or delusional: Do people around you give you confirming feedback that you're really good? That combination—your own feeling of being capable, combined with confirmation from others—is a great clue to which color is your most natural approach.

chapter ten

STACK THE RUSSIAN NESTING DOLLS

Do you know that sinking feeling, the one you get when a friend or a boss announces it's time to make a change—and then describes a plan that is essentially the same as the last six plans? As this person earnestly commits to innovating in the same way as always, perhaps adding a promise to "try harder," you already know how it's going to turn out. That's a discouraging moment, but what I want to point out is that this person *is trying* to innovate. That's a key point: When a person fails to innovate, it is rarely because that person had no approach to innovation or made no effort. It's because he or she is stuck in an outdated or exhausted way of trying to be new. In terms of prismatic thinking, innovation fails when the innovator is focused on only one of the four approaches to innovation, rather than considering all the options. The key is not just to try something new, but to try a new and better way of trying something new. To succeed, we have to innovate how we innovate.

You might ask: Why? Why can't we keep doing the kind of innovation we're good at, the kind we feel comfortable with? Why can't each of us just find our favorite strategy and stick with it? The answer is that while innovation involves a relationship with ourselves, that's not all it involves. Naturally, the *decision* to renew some part of your life is personal. We say: *I'm* unhappy. *I* see a chance to make things better. *I* have a dream. I, I, I. But what begins as a conversation with the self can't end there. I see so many people get so caught up in the question of "What kind of person am I?" and "What's my style?" that they miss the rest of innovation. The simple recipe at the heart of so many self-help books is essentially "to thine own self be true." All there is to making your life new and improved, they say, is a simple three-step checklist:

1. Figure out what comes naturally to you.
2. Do more of it.
3. Live happily ever after.

That's not terrible advice. In fact, it's essential, but it isn't enough. It's a fantasy to think it's that simple. And if that's all you've got, you are in for disappointment and heartbreak.

understand different levels of you

When Aruna was young, her parents emphasized achievement, but they also encouraged her to follow her heart. In college she majored in art history, her favorite subject, but when she graduated she found herself with few job possibilities, and those she found paid poorly and gave her little in the way of challenge. After two discouraging years, she took her parents' advice and continued reluctantly on to law school, where she graduated with distinction. She married Rajeev, a medical student, and joined a law firm. They appeared to be a model high-achieving young couple.

Unfortunately, Aruna found life at the law firm overwhelming. She worked constantly, was never given sufficient time to properly prep her cases, and was frequently berated by the overachieving partners who had sacrificed their personal lives for the benefit of the practice. To compound matters, her husband, now a medical resident, was constantly on call at the hospital. They had very little time together. When she joined her colleagues after work for a beer, they would lament about their mean-spirited taskmasters, but they also seemed to find the sweatshop experience strangely exhilarating. They didn't miss going to museums and galleries the way Aruna did. They didn't seem to feel that they'd left real life behind. She felt alone and despondent.

One day, Aruna was assigned to a project with a seasoned attorney named Chetana. Chetana was also Indian and admitted that employment among the white-shoe boys could be tiresome, even though the situation had improved considerably over the years. They met to discuss their case every other day over afternoon tea. When Aruna confided that she was seriously considering leaving the firm, Chetana observed how similar the two were and encouraged her to find ways of incorporating her personal interests into her work and to stay on until she reached partner.

Aruna was reenergized by the friendship, finding in it a symbolic promise that there might be a place for her at the firm after all. She worked diligently. The demanding case dragged on for over a year before it was successfully settled in a dramatic flurry of round-the-clock work. The firm gave Aruna a few days off to recover, and she used some of the time to write up a business plan, which she presented to Chetana as soon as she returned. In the plan she proposed that the firm add an art litigation practice, to give the company a new line of business and to let her integrate her personal passion for art into her work. She asked Chetana to bring the plan to the senior partners.

This is where you might find the fantasy I mentioned earlier. In the fantasy version, the story would go something like this: Chetana, now playing the role of fairy godmother, takes the business plan to the senior partners and waves her magic wand. The hard-driving partners suddenly relax and smile. They are delighted with the proposal, and offer to support Aruna as she launches the new practice area. In this fairy-tale version, the moral of the story is that Aruna has learned to be herself—and after that, everything falls into place.

Sadly, that wasn't what happened. After hearing Aruna's proposal, Chetana smiled sympathetically, took a deep breath, and said, "I'm sorry, but I can't take this to the partners. We both know they'll never go for it. That sort of thing just isn't a priority around here." Silent and heartbroken, Aruna left her office, and three days later she quit the firm. Chetana called and left a warm invitation to talk, but Aruna never returned the call.

What was the problem here? Let's take out the prism and think through the colors. Aruna was at a top law firm, a Compete environment, intensely blue, and she had the Compete training to do what was asked of her. But although she could keep up with the blues, Aruna was not a blue herself. The winning-is-everything life didn't thrill her. It stifled her. However, the firm succeeded by outcompeting other firms and its leaders didn't care if Aruna was being true to herself or not. They cared about how many hours she could bill. Back at school, there had been time for both Compete and Create activities, but in the high-pressure world of the firm she was forced to make a choice.

What Aruna was discovering the hard way was that it's not enough to discover your preferred innovation style and stick to it, because the work of remaking our lives extends beyond us. It's as if there are several different versions of us, acting at different levels. To picture this complex reality—that we exist on three different levels at once—I like to imagine that people are really matryoshka dolls, the Russian nesting dolls: Each version of us is stacked inside the next, the same face and body but on a different scale: small, medium, or large. Each of us is an independent individual, master of our own fate, yet we are also a member of one or more families, businesses, and other communities. We are also citizens of a country, actors in a global market, and a part of what people call the universe or God's creation. We exist on all three levels at the same time, and each level has some claim on us, setting some limits and offering some opportunities as we try to shape our fate. Let's look more closely at the three levels.

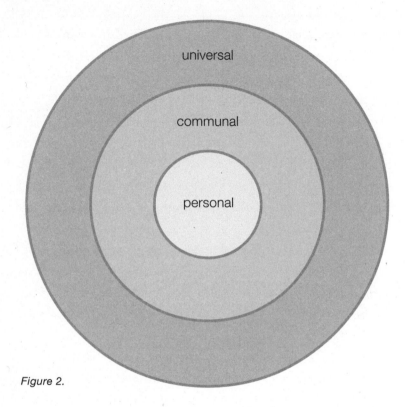

Figure 2.

the universal level

The biggest nesting doll exists at the "universal" level: It describes you in relationship to those universal forces that are too big for any of us to control. We name these forces nature, markets, technologies, society, and God if we are believers. I think of this as the "it" level. This universal "it" acts on us, but we do not act on it—you can't reach out your arms and stop a hurricane. When China challenges the United State for economic dominance, when changing climate

patterns lead to flooding around the world, when a wave of funda-
mentalism or of reform changes the political reality, individuals and
communities feel the impact at the universal level.

Acknowledging that we exist in part on the universal level is one
way my approach differs from psychological-type indicators. I may
be an introvert or an extrovert, a feeling person or a thinking person, but the stock market and the global climate and the political
winds of change don't care. When there are changes on the universal
level, I have no choice but to observe and to respond. That's one
reason, as I suggested in Step I, that there is no data on the future:
We can't know all of the big changes that will touch us. And we can
only compensate for them by committing to watch the weather, to
ride what moves, and to experiment with our own approach in
response.

the communal level

Looking inside the "universal" doll, we find the middle-sized doll,
which describes the communal level, the level of "we." At this level
we exist in relationships to communities of all kinds, such as families,
businesses, schools, sports organizations, and houses of worship.
These communities offer chances to express our desires, values, and
beliefs as part of a group. They also offer some protection from the
largest level, such as pooling resources when the financial market
falls, and some chance to benefit from the enormous changes at the
universal level. Your community can function as a safety net or a soft
landing spot, providing you support when you need it. At the communal level we can have some impact on our own fate by asking:
Who do I know? Who could I partner with? How does what I want
connect to what others need?

the personal level

Inside your "communal" doll, the individual or "I" doll is the smallest doll of the three, describing your relationship to yourself: your body, values, dreams, personal intelligence, and skills, as well as physical health and mental health. If you don't have satisfaction at this level, the rest won't matter, but if you only focus on innovating at the personal level, you will never find long-term success and satisfaction. The most dangerous delusion we suffer from as we try to innovate our lives is that the individual level is enough. Especially in America, I think there is a tendency to imagine that if one is true enough to oneself, committed enough, talented enough, self-improved and self-discovered and spiritually in touch, then the other levels won't matter.

You can see the kind of tragedies that result from this misunderstanding in many places, including on social networks. Increasingly I hear stories of Facebook affairs, in which people who are disappointed with their lives reconnect with an old flame on a social networking site and then make sudden, highly risky life decisions—to leave their current spouse or town, to turn their lives upside down, and to reunite with someone they've "never stopped thinking about," even though the thinking they have been doing may not have changed since they were seventeen. It's very romantic, but the danger is that the two people newly in love will forget they exist on the other two levels (the universal and the communal) as well.

The person who seemed perfect for you way back when may have made very different commitments than you have in terms of work, family, and hopes for the future. The cost of leaving behind your own family, job, or hometown is almost certain to be far higher than it would have been decades ago, when you had so much less to lose. No one level of the three is enough for the long term, even when you are in love, although love can be enormously helpful as you work to innovate your life on all three levels. So I don't mean to prejudge this hypothetical late-summer romance, only to encourage the romantics to stack the proverbial nesting dolls before they turn their feelings into commitments.

The wisdom of the nesting dolls is not that communal always trumps personal. Sometimes the personal trumps the communal, as Aruna discovered the hard way. What Aruna hadn't considered, even when she found she could not be satisfied with purely Compete success, was that being true to her preferred individual approach only took care of the smallest doll, the "I." For that reason, while each of us may feel that one of the four colors "comes naturally"—and even though in this book I will say that someone "is" a Compete, a Create, a Collaborate, or a Control—prismatic thinking also requires us to look at all three levels together, to "stack the Russian nesting dolls" and make sure none has gotten lost.

look up, down, and around

It should be clearer now why I began with the creativize method, encouraging you to watch the weather, light your fires where sparks fly, and so on—the innovator's stance ensures that you are watching the opportunities and risks at all three levels. As you plan your efforts to remake your life, at each step along the way, it's necessary to check all three levels. To me, this is the innovator's mantra: *Look up, down, and around.*

That's what Aruna couldn't do. With her tight focus on the level of self, her own personal needs for a life that was not just blue but also green, she was blindsided by the decision of the law firm, which operated at the communal level by its own communal rules, which were strictly blue.

So what happened to Aruna? After weeks of second-guessing, she accepted an offer from a family friend who was making a success of an art gallery in Soho. Taking an enormous pay cut, she settled into a job where she could talk about art all day long. She enjoyed her work, but found it moved more slowly than her work at the law firm. The slow pace left her a lot of time to consider her regrets, and she began to feel that she had made a terrible mistake in going to law school at all. Her husband was fully consumed with being a doctor, and Aruna worried that she had missed her chance to build a career as her husband was doing, one that challenged her every day, where her work could be recognized and rewarded.

Several months later, she received a phone call from Chetana, asking if she would be interested in assisting with a new case as a freelance member of her team. The firm was representing a Latin American museum that was suing a deposed dictator to recover jewelry and other treasures of historical significance. At first, Aruna hesitated. Did she really want to go back to the organization that had disappointed her so badly? On reflection, though, she realized that she was not going back all the way. It was only one case. She could even reduce her hours at the gallery a little and do both.

Aruna joined the team and to her surprise she found the work engaging. She was shocked by how much she now liked collaborating with her old colleagues from the law firm in these changed circumstances, and amazed that she enjoyed using the legal training she had recently been wishing away. With encouragement from Chetana and Rajeev, she set out to form her own boutique legal practice, specializing in matters of art and limited to cases that interested her. She came to see that she was neither simply a blue nor simply a green, but also that to express her hybrid nature she needed a community that welcomed both, a community she would never find at a big, prestigious law firm. Aruna had learned to be true to herself and at the same time to recognize the limits of her former community, the firm. Rather than accepting the harsh choice she faced, she had innovated an alternative. She had stacked the Russian nesting dolls by recognizing that she could create her own hybrid at the community level—her boutique firm—to match her personal hybrid nature, a mix of "Compete" and "Create."

chapter eleven

———

HOW YOU INNOVATE
IS WHAT YOU INNOVATE

Poor Caroline. Remember her? We left her behind a couple of chapters ago, overwhelmed by options. Her ailing father needed better and more expensive nursing care, and I talked to her about all the different possibilities for innovating. She understood that she had to use the prism and consider all four colors. She knew that when she considered the four colors, she had to do so not just in terms of what suited her personally, at the level of self, but also in terms of the larger "nesting dolls" that influenced her life: the people and organizations at the community level and the larger forces beyond anyone's control. Finally, though, she started to lose patience. Four colors, three levels—how many possibilities were we creating now? Wasn't there a way to focus on the best choice, or at least the best two or three choices? After all we were still only talking about her overall *approach* to innovation. We hadn't even gotten to specific actions she could take. Wasn't there some practical way to pick her best approach to innovation?

The most important thing to know about innovation—and the most important idea in this book—is that the approach is not just a matter of style. The approach is everything: How you work on your life determines what changes you can get. If you focus on closing more deals faster, your heightened competitiveness may make you wealthier, but it will never bring new creations into being or gather a community around you and help you discover the meaning in life. Heading north will never get you south. Getting straight A's will never make you a professional dancer. How you innovate is what you innovate.

Many people get it backward. They decide how they feel like innovating and then hope it gets them to their goal. Caroline, as I've said, was most comfortable with a red or Control approach. Control innovations can make you safer, preserve your savings, and systematically achieve goals without a lot of risk. And so she continued to track her monthly budget and cut down on unnecessary spending and work with her own hands, but trimming here and pitching in there could never solve her underlying problem. She was like British Petroleum when the oil well exploded in the Gulf of Mexico—trying to meet this year's challenge with last year's solution.

So how to pick a better approach? The best way to pick your approach is to start with your goals and work backward from there. Just as there are only four approaches to innovation, there are only two main benefits to each one, making a total of eight goals. If you know which one or two you want most, you can use that as your guide.

COLLABORATE APPROACH (yellow)

1. Capability: This approach can make you more capable through learning and intellectual development. *For Caroline that might mean taking nursing courses to become a better caregiver.*
2. Community: This approach can connect you with community: family, friends, colleague, and customers. *For Caroline, that could mean trying to reconnect with other family members who would share the burden of her father's care, though she had not had much success with this approach in the past.*

CREATE APPROACH (green)

3. Creativity: This approach invents things that are new or radically different: original vision and artistic expression. *For Caroline, that could mean inventing a new career for herself.*

4. Discovery: This approach leads to psychological and spiritual insight. *For Caroline, this could mean investigating the underlying psychological reasons she was struggling to provide for her father and herself.*

COMPETE APPROACH (blue)

5. Vitality: This approach benefits your physical and emotional health. *For Caroline, vitality wasn't an issue—she was fortunate to be healthy and her mental focus was good.*

6. Prosperity: This approach deals with financial well-being. *For Caroline, more money would mean she could cover her increased expenses.*

CONTROL APPROACH (red)

7. Security: This approach ensures safety and maximizes savings. *This was what Caroline had already tried, but she could go even further, making drastic reductions in her spending and drastic changes in her lifestyle.*

8. Productivity: This approach puts systems in place to make you more consistently successful at what you do. *Caroline was already a systematic worker and was successful in meeting the challenges she set for herself.*

Looking over this list, Caroline quickly noted a few possible benefits of innovation that seemed irrelevant or unhelpful to her situation or that she had already tried. She crossed Discovery, Vitality, and Productivity off her list. Then she crossed off Security because that was the method she was trying already and the idea of cutting her spending much more would mean completely upending her life. Even after she crossed off four of these eight benefits, though, she still had too many choices. Which was most important?

There are natural tensions among some of the innovation approaches. Caroline had already discovered one herself: She could spend more time making money to pay for her father's care (blue) or she could spend more time learning to care for her father and caring for him personally (yellow), but she couldn't be both at work more and at home more. Both of these results would be valuable to her, but they were competing with each other—more of one almost always means less of the other. (That's why my colleagues and I called our original business model the *Competing* Values Framework.)

There are two questions that can help you spotlight the competing needs of opposite approaches and see the natural trade-offs in order to to make clear which is more important for you. These questions ask you to describe the kind of innovation you need: (a) How fast do you need this innovation to work? (b) How much innovation do you need—big changes or small?

how fast?

There is a natural tension between the Compete and Collaborate (blue and yellow) forms of innovation. This tension comes down to a basic decision about time: How fast does your innovation need to happen? You can see this tension in any business in the world. In larger companies it shows up as the perennial tension between the human resources people and the finance people. Their fight comes down to a question of goals: Is our priority to train and retain the best possible employees or is it to be as profitable as possible this quarter? If we want to develop our community, the human resources people always say, we're going to have to spend more and be patient about seeing results—otherwise the company has no future in the long term. But if we want to record a profit in the short term, the finance people respond, we need to cut back expenditures such as training and support for our people. In corporate terms: Do we pursue sustainable organizational competencies and culture, which take time to develop, or do we pursue a short-term opportunity, which must be acted upon quickly? Are we going to emphasize speed or sustainability?

For Caroline, the answer was clear. She'd already spent a lot of money she didn't mean to spend. She needed her innovation to show results quickly. So in the inevitable trade-off between Compete and Collaborate, she was leaning toward Compete.

how much?

There is a similar tension involving the Create and Control approaches, based on the size of change you need in your life and the amount of risk you're willing to take on. All businesses must make a choice: Do we pursue revolutionary innovation, which brings great risk and expense, or do we pursue incremental and scalable innovation, which has less risk but often lacks sufficient inventiveness to develop new markets? For example, most start-up biotech firms risk everything they've got to develop novel drug therapies, because they are too small to compete against the big pharmaceutical companies in any other way. An established pharmaceutical company, however, can afford to focus on developing relatively minor enhancements. If they can make a slightly better drug, one that improves its patients' lives even a small amount, and then sell millions of doses of that drug, they will still see a healthy profit, but without risking the future of the company, as the small start-ups have to do.

For an individual, the equivalent question is: Do you need a little something new in your life? Or do you need a whole new life? How ambitious are you? Let's say you have always enjoyed throwing pottery and you dream of giving up your day job for the life of a craftsperson. If you would be happy to improve your craft a little and perhaps sell your work locally, you could take classes at the nearby art school and keep the rest of your life in place. Low risk, small reward, though perhaps over time you could build to bigger success. On the other hand, if you could quit your job and leave town, you could travel to one of the top schools in the country for a master of fine arts in ceramics. You would see many advantages, but the risk would be big: You would have to give up your job, leave your home, and cut yourself off from your community. Big risk, but the possibility of big reward, sooner.

Caroline looked at her situation. Did she need to make a change fast or could it be slow? Fast. Did she need a big change or could it be small and incremental? Big change. Those answers pointed her toward blue and green. Now she looked again at the benefits still on her list: between Prosperity (blue) and Creative invention (green), which was her priority? Definitely Prosperity. Now she had her answer: To innovate her way to a better life, her approach needed to be primarily blue.

Once she knew what her approach needed to be, she considered the nesting blocks. At the universal level, given the economy, was it going to be possible to be more competitive as a real estate agent? If not, she was going to have to get Creative—she would need to turn toward green. But although the real estate market was down for both new homes and sales of existing homes, Caroline had been watching the weather and looking to ride what moved. The overall real estate market was down, but with so many people unwilling or unable to leave their homes, and prices falling, the market for summer homes in her area was heating up. In Caroline's area there was something of a boom—a practical opportunity at the level of community. Her boss had even asked her to take on more work.

She had told him at the time that she couldn't do it, given her family commitments. But now when she talked with her father about her new "blue" approach, he agreed—sometimes, he told her, the best way to take care of your family was to focus on your own career. The truth was, this approach made Caroline somewhat uncomfortable on the personal level, but at this point she was even more concerned about her father and her financial future. To put it in technical terms, her life sucked, and she could feel risk and reward reverse. If what she and her father needed was for her to increase her income so that she could afford to place him in an assisted-living facility, she was willing to try. She would blend her natural Control approach with a Compete approach. She had made her decision.

chapter twelve

THE MOST POWERFUL APPROACH
TO INNOVATION

Dan served in the military police in Asia, an enormously challenging job. He had to keep control of drunk, angry, and aggressive soldiers in the barracks using only his hands and a billy club. He learned to do it the way his local counterparts did, by mastering karate. When his tour of duty ended and he came back to America, he continued his karate practice, joining a strict dojo like the one where he had first trained. He loved how the practice gave him confidence and discipline, how it kept his body in shape and his mind in focus. In time, when he tired of the kind of bodyguard work he could get with his military background, he decided to move back to his hometown and open his own dojo to share the skills that had served him so well.

Dan was eager to pass on the tradition he had learned, a demanding approach based on self-discipline, obedience, respect, and rigorous testing—in Competing Values terms, the sport was extreme red. As a business matter, however, Dan soon found that he had a problem. In his small city, karate was not an area of growth for adults. Even with aggressive local marketing, he was barely breaking even. But while he struggled to find enough adult students, he found that many families with no martial arts background were looking for training for their children. He realized that to ride what moved, he would need to take on children as students.

Dan felt thrilled at the chance to share his practice with a younger generation, but the kids were not thrilled. They were miserable. Many hated the focus on discipline, repetition, and obedience to short, sharp commands. They cried and cried. Then their parents asked for refunds.

Dan might have concluded that a "red" sport could not be taught to small children, who are naturally Creative and Collaborative—green and yellow. He might have decided that American culture was not a fit for his sport. Was this a case where one of the four competing values destroys another, and no compromise is possible?

Dan talked to a business coach who advised him to start over again in a bigger city where he could fill a dojo with adult students. However, the kids' unhappy reactions had spoken to something inside him. Back when he had been new to karate, he had found his early training a grueling, painful, and humiliating experience, a kind of authorized hazing, sanctioned abuse. Had he not needed the skills so desperately to use on the job, he might well have quit. And although he had ultimately survived and excelled, he also remembered the times when he had felt as bad on the inside as some of the crying children in his dojo.

Instead of packing up his business and taking it to a bigger city, he began to think around the colors and across the levels of the nesting dolls. *How fast* did he need his innovation to work? He had enough customers to keep him afloat, barely, and a business line of credit: His situation was not an emergency. The changes he needed did not have to come right away. *How big* an innovation did he need? He needed a major innovation. Incremental "red" adjustments that might increase his student body by a small percentage each year were not going to make his business profitable. Cost-cutting and improved efficiency wouldn't help either—he needed to be in an accessible location and he needed talented teachers, so there was no way to make dramatic reductions in his rent or his payroll. Becoming more competitive about marketing was only going to cause more of the same problem he had already: Lots of interested parents would bring their kids, then the kids would cry and the parents would ask for their money back.

Dan needed a new approach, a new vision, a new way of connecting to the community of possible students. He realized he needed to become more of a Create so he could invent a new way to reach his Collaborate goal: understanding and working with his community. Dan knew very little about teaching children, but his city had a good college that offered adult education classes. He began to study child development. He took classes in psychology and sought out local experts who understood kids.

One day it hit him—instead of trying to get his kids to accept traditional karate culture, he had to create a new culture that would welcome them as they were, a new, yellow way of learning karate. He began to experiment. He kept the rigorous testing and the focus on respect, but instead of motivating with authority and humiliation, he learned to motivate with encouragement, respect, and love. He required parents to participate in the program—not to practice karate, but to add their attention and their moral support.

As he began to have success, he worked with his teachers to write his own guidebook and in time created his own line of homemade videos. He lost some of his most traditional students, but not many. And as word spread, he attracted large numbers of new students. His dojo became one of the most successful in the area, and he became known as one of the top teachers for black belt certification, and his kids were happy to be there.

Dan's successful change of his approach is instructive. He didn't simply change colors, shifting from red to yellow to reach his goal. He created a new hybrid of colors, combining traditional "red" martial arts and contemporary American "yellow" child psychology in a practical "blue" business plan. His innovation was not just a profitable new karate school located in a small midwestern city, it was a new approach to martial arts overall. And like the most powerful innovations, the innovation was not just the thing he built (the dojo) but the capability he invented that made it work. Think of Apple: The iPod was not a breakthrough—there were many other digital music players before it that never became breakaway successes. But in addition to the iPod, Apple developed iTunes, which gave users the capability to do things with a digital player that they had never done, and very much wanted to do. In time, as we all know, the iPod gave way to the iPhone and the iPad. What makes them all valuable is what you can do on each of them, easily and effectively, through iTunes: The innovations are at least as much in the capability as in the machine.

create your hybrid approach

The most powerful innovations don't just replace one approach with another; they create a new hybrid approach that enables a new capability. Aruna didn't just quit the competitive law firm to join the creative world of art; she found a way to combine her "blue" training with her "green" calling. And these hybrid approaches can be developed at all three levels.

It might be hard to remember now—when everyone from football players to politicians will wear pink to raise awareness of breast cancer—that the topic of breast cancer used to be a humiliating secret, whispered about privately and with shame. The movement to bring it out of hiding and unite efforts to find a cure started like most movement: small, intimate, and, in this case, tragic.

A young woman from Peoria, Illinois, named Susan Goodman Komen was diagnosed with the disease. Through a series of missteps her condition worsened and eventually consumed her. After her death, her younger sister, Nancy Goodman Brinker, founded the Susan G. Komen for the Cure organization to support research and treatment for breast cancer. It began as a local, grassroots effort, but sometimes luck shows her favor as ideas find their place in time. Betty Ford, the wife of the former president, who less than a decade earlier had gone public about her mastectomy, pushed to make October National Breast Cancer Month. Millions of women identified with her story, which, like Susan's, was so personal, harrowing, and yet universal. Communities began holding the Komen Race for the Cure in October, a five-kilometer fitness walk to raise funds, celebrate survivors, and memorialize the fallen. These events became happenings like rock concerts, drawing huge numbers of engaged participants, all wearing pink. Pink began to appear on all manner of products and services. Estée Lauder led the charge with their pink ribbon crusade. Soon fashion designers and health food companies and even football teams joined the cause. Something had changed in America. This most common and dreaded disease had gone from being a forbidden topic to a single-color megabrand—pink. The Cure had become everyone's battle.

These products appealed to our hearts, but the business model was sound: A percentage of revenues from all "pink" products went to the Susan G. Komen for the Cure organization. Not only was the organization able to raise millions for breast cancer research, but a new model for organizations began to emerge, one that connected philanthropy to for-profit commerce. The organization became something new: a profitable not-for-profit. They called this hybrid approach "cause-related marketing." A traditional yellow movement had become a powerful yellow-blue hybrid.

How do you create these powerful hybrids? The first step is to creativize as I have described, thinking around the colors and stacking all three levels of the Russian nesting blocks, to revise your approach to innovation based on your goals and your awareness of the forces operating all around you. When you have that new vision of your approach—the combination of colors that could help you reach your goals—then the time has come to experiment to find the specific methods that will turn an approach into a success. That's the subject of Step III of this book. But before we get there I want to point out two dangers that sabotage many innovators before they even get to the stage of making practical attempts.

chapter thirteen

CREATE CAPACITY — EMPTY THE BAG

Why is it that every year, so many sincere people make New Year's resolutions, only to watch those sincere commitments fade away? All those promises to get to the gym more, to make time (finally) to finish that dream project, to get out of town to enjoy the country more or to get into town to see a museum or a show, and a million other well-intentioned plans wind up on the shelf for another year. I often hear people blame a lack of commitment or willpower. I also hear a lot about the complex and demanding schedules of our twenty-first-century lives, but often the true explanation is both simpler and more insidious. Often our attempts to renew our lives fall short because we have no room: in our schedules and, even more important, in our minds. Our lives are like bags too full to hold even one more thing. We can make all the promises we like; we have no room to innovate.

When the stock market crashed, many panicked MBA students at the University of Michigan came to me for advice. They said: My job search is going badly, but Jeff, you know all these people in New York, northern California—would you help me? Of course, students have always gone to their professors to find help with employment. The trouble was the baggage these students were carrying. Several told me that their dream job was working for a well-known design and innovation consulting firm founded in Palo Alto or other big names in New York. But even though their credentials and qualifications looked good, they were not offered the jobs they wanted. The weather had changed. The summer was over. It was not enough for them to look for jobs in well-known places or in a conventional way. I said: You're going to have to think about this differently.

Couldn't I help them at all? they asked. I said yes, I can. In fact, I can help you create exactly the career you want. I can help you get a job in the innovation industry just as you hope. I just can't do it the way you have in mind. You have to think about the big changes we can't control and the communities that still have opportunities. Can you let go of getting your first job in one of those "really cool" cities? If you can empty the bag of that idea, there are jobs to be had in locales you haven't thought about. There's a furniture maker down south, for instance, that needs to reinvent itself or go under. That would be a fabulous place for you to start out, because the company is small enough that you'll have influence right away on big decisions, and they'll give you stock options, which means that if they make it big, so will you.

I kept having these conversations. I said: I'm happy to help you— now let's talk about jobs in Louisville. Let's talk about jobs in Little Rock. But every one of my students had the same response. Crestfallen, they said, "But I don't want to live in a place like that!" And of course, there were still jobs in the typically desirable cities—just not jobs for freshly graduated MBAs doing the kind of work that these students had hoped and trained to do. So they had a choice. Something had to come out of the bag. Either they could have the job they wanted in an unexpected place or a job they didn't want in the place where they expected to go.

This wasn't just me giving my students a hard time. As I said earlier, Marshall McLuhan, one of the great visionaries on innovation, wrote that innovation *enhances something*, making it better or new. But he also said that innovation *eliminates or destroys something*.

Just as Wikipedia made research faster and more convenient, it also discouraged other forms of research—not just traditional library research but even Google searches.

Even Santa Claus, our beloved icon of gain without pain, has to empty his sack so that he can fill it with new gifts next year. Every approach to innovation costs something—every kind of creation involves creative destruction—which is why some of the most effective decisions to enable innovation are more about stopping current practices than starting new ones. You just can't afford to carry around commitments and attitudes that don't help you reach your innovation goals. No one can. If you want to be a more involved parent, you're going to have to come home more, show up at school more, and be there for your child's performances and events more than someone who isn't a parent or doesn't share your goal. And if you're at home and at school more, you'll be at work less. At times, you will miss out on professional opportunities because you're not there to seize them or because you don't have the energy left to take on one more project. You will make less money than if you were not also trying to be more involved in your child's life. That doesn't mean someone can't be a professional success and a good parent, but there is no way to maximize both at the same time. The same goes for being a great friend, a great soul mate, a great patron of your local theater company—every collaborative commitment has a cost in competitive focus. (There's a reason investment bankers' wives jokingly refer to themselves as investment bank widows.) There is no escaping the tension between Compete and Collaborate; between blue and yellow, there are only different ways of responding to it in order to find what you need in order to grow.

In the same way, if you want to become a marathon runner, you're going to have to give up a great deal of your time. There are training runs, workouts. You'll need extra sleep so that the body can respond to the new strain you've put it under. You'll need time to care for the inevitable injuries. You'll feel a great deal of pressure to change the way you eat, how much alcohol you drink, a whole list of comforts and pleasures, changes that will take you away from people who are not altering their lives.

Each new goal puts pressure on us to stop doing some of what we already do. In our postmodern life, however, we have a hard time saying no to what we're doing. We hate to burn our bridges or take options off the table. Big companies love to start projects and announce fresh initiatives, but they hate to stop old ones. Starting means new prestige, new attention, and new reasons for people to love the company. Stopping means disappointing people, admitting failure, fighting political battles. It's easier just to launch more new initiatives on top of all the previous initiatives, but if they don't empty the bag, those initiatives may be doomed from the start.

At the personal level, almost anyone you know will tell you that they are overly busy and overly stressed, but who controls that? The person saying so. So we suffer with our "do it all" mentality and inadvertently create a mélange of mediocrity. Trying to have it all, all at the same time, is at best difficult, and, at worst, destructive.

I feel I can deliver this news with confidence because I've walked the walk. When I received my PhD, I was offered an Ivy League professorship, but I turned it down to take a job with a small pizza chain in the middle of the country. Instead of buying a pretty house on the East Coast, I went back to the Midwest to think about making and delivering pizza pies. Believe me, you get a very different response at parties if your first line is, "I'm a professor at an Ivy League school," rather than, "I work for a pizza company." I gave up a lot of prestige. I gave up the security of tenure for the risk of entrepreneurship. I emptied the bag. I did it because at that pizza company, a twenty-million-dollar regional success, I could do the innovation work I wanted to do. And we built Domino's into a multibillion-dollar global juggernaut: The company was the Google of the 1980s.

Remaking your life is inherently about effective trade-offs. Are you willing to give something up to gain what you seek? As you formulate your new approach to innovation for whatever goal is most important to you right now, ask yourself: What are you willing right now to stop doing? What is it you will phase out slowly or stop today? And are you willing to put that commitment on the calendar?

When you have an idea of what you can give up, apply what I think of as the Lent test. I'm a Roman Catholic, and at Lent we are instructed to give up something to help us let in something more important—we make room for God. But what we give up has to be something big enough in our lives to clear some serious space. It has to be something that matters, personally. Before someone decides, "For Lent, I'm giving up chocolate," they need to ask themselves: Do I *really* like chocolate? Because if not, it's not going to empty the bag, not much. So ask yourself: What is it you are attached to that doesn't serve your goal? Shopping discount deal sites? Playing videogames? Whatever it may be, if you're giving it your time and energy and resources, then that's a great choice for emptying the bag.

Depending on your dominant innovation color, you will likely find that you have corresponding areas you resist giving up. I'm sorry to say, these are the things you need to give up most, for a time, in order for your new approach to innovations to succeed:

- Yellows resist giving up their friendships, their allies, their communities. They keep working with people even when the partnerships stop being productive. They try to make everyone happy. Their awareness of people's emotional needs distracts them from their goals.
- Greens don't like to give up freedom. They want to leave the door open to one more new alternative, one more new idea. They don't like to fill up their calendars or commit to due dates and arrangements with fixed consequences.
- Blues hate to give up money. There is a blue who works for me who couldn't stand the time I put into writing this book. I turned down business to clear time in my schedule,

and it drove him crazy. He said, "This is money we're talk-ing about!" And I had to say, "Yeah, you're exactly right, but everything costs something."

- Reds are hard-pressed to give up their responsibilities. They cling to their authority, their procedures, their sense that things must be done in a certain way and to a certain standard. Caroline, the real estate broker who wanted to live as more of a blue, realized that she spent too much time on each house she sold. She was too particular about how it should look, too involved in working through her checklists with her clients. She had to let some of her care-ful routines go and use the time to take on more clients.

Can't we have it all? Actually, we can. As a practical matter, innova-tion can ultimately lead us to everything we want. We just can't have it all *right now*. As the yogis suggest, the little mustard seed really does contain the entire tree inside of it, but it requires favorable con-ditions and time to fulfill its potential. Our goals are the same. At the end of the book, in Step IV, I explain how the cycles of innovation can make it possible to reach all of your goals—but for now, I ask you to empty the bag of your wish to have it all, focus on putting your new approach into practice, and come back to that question in its time.

chapter fourteen

—

AVOID THE NEGATIVE ZONE

As a young man, Mickey was quick, creative, and slippery. He took every shortcut possible, and he seemed to think the rules didn't apply to him. Throughout high school, it worked for him. In spite of the fast cars and late parties, he managed to keep up decent grades, wowing his teachers with his unusual mind or charming them with his confident style. He was captain of the swim team and the first in his family to get into college. Then, just weeks before he was supposed to leave for college, he was arrested with two friends for selling drugs, an offense that landed him in the county jail for two months and tattooed a felony on his record that would haunt him for years. His college didn't want him anymore. Everyone in town had seen his story in the local news, and many said that now Mickey was going to have to learn to play by the rules just like everyone else.

What did he do? He decided he was nothing like everyone else. He didn't need an ordinary life. For years, he slipped from city to city, working as a waiter at fine restaurants where his past wouldn't be an issue, telling people he was a novelist or that he was working on a plan to start his own business. At first he loved the life of pleasure: after-hours parties when he got off work and a new girlfriend at every turn. Though the locations changed, the characters in his life didn't—charming addicts, liars, and thieves. It seemed it would last forever, but one day he woke up in his thirties, exhausted and broke, with no future and a long list of friends who had self-destructed. He came home to live in his brother Kellen's basement. Kellen, a successful entrepreneur, had never given up on him.

Mickey had gone over to what I call the negative zone. He was a Create, a green, who rejected all the rules and restrictions of his opposite color, red. He was so deep into being a green that he had no other resources to draw on for fashioning a life. Lacking any structure or sense of obligation, his creativity burned off in pointless rebellion and vague experimentation. With only one color to draw on, he could not create any kind of functional blend.

Inside the negative zone, it doesn't feel like a problem or a mistake. It often feels more like safety, like righteous commitment, sometimes even like following orders and sticking to the plan. In the negative zone, the problem is not how to "empty the bag," it's that the bag is too empty—in a sense, it has a hole in it, and most of the colors have seeped out.

All four colors have a negative zone. Harry was a Control, a successful marketing manager whose company went under. After some hard months of fruitless job searching, he found a consulting job out of town. On his first day, his boss told him: Here are the five things we need to do to move this company forward. They were approaches Harry had used at his previous job, and he could see right away how he would adapt them for his new boss. He drove the two hours back home feeling confident. Reds are the best people for taking one approach and improving it, incrementally, for different but related uses.

Over two years, working from home a couple of hours away, Harry helped his new company grow. But as the company thrived, their needs changed. Harry's boss started sending him requests for new approaches, but Harry would write marketing proposals that looked like the old approaches. When his boss rejected these, he'd work twice as hard, writing more pages in greater detail, but still with the same underlying approaches. Harry had gone into the negative zone as a Control.

For the first time, Harry's proposals began to fail. He lost business to competitors. His boss was furious. In an angry conference call, his boss ordered him to move to a nearby city so he could be part of the company culture and conversation. Harry was reluctant. That wasn't how he did things—he had a family where he lived and he wasn't going to move them. A two-hour commute, he thought, would disrupt his entire life. Harry also resisted requests to be in more frequent contact with new members of the company. He thought that his success was based on his ability to continually refine his skills instead of learning something new or adopting a different approach. The company was growing and changing, with frequent and intense conversations among senior management. Yet increasingly, Harry worked on his own in his basement home-office, and his work became increasingly irrelevant. At the moment he most needed to listen to alternatives, he kept on going the same way as always, letting the growing crisis in his work life push him back to the innovation approach that made him feel most comfortable. He complained ceaselessly about what had happened to the company—they were unfair to him, they had lost their focus, they wouldn't give him a shot. He preserved his way of doing things and his settled life, and when his boss was hired away by another company, he found that no one else remembered his past successes. His contract was not renewed. He had been working as hard as ever, but he had become irrelevant.

Most of us slip into the negative zone at least some of the time. Under stress or when we face too much criticism or too many competing demands, we retreat into our most settled approaches to innovation and our favorite complaints about the world, screening out every point of view but our own. In the negative zone, we stop self-authorizing and fall back into the reactionary mode, all criticism: "These people don't understand me." "No one ever gives me a chance." "They're all crazy/wrong/biased/stupid." The negative zone doesn't usually feel like going to extremes—it may even feel like coming home or holding tight to your principles. But as comfortable as you are in your private certainty, you may be able to detect damage in the area opposite your color. Mickey never questioned his creativity or his entitlement to be free to follow his sense of what was right, but as unpaid bills piled up and friends wound up in rehab, in jail, or in the ground, he could see that his life was out of control, without shape or accomplishments to show for it. He could feel the cost of trying to make a life with no red at all. That was part of what drove him to swallow his pride and ask his successful brother to take him in.

Kellen gave Mickey a low-level administrative job in his firm, on one condition: Mickey had to attend night school at the local community college. Mickey found that he actually enjoyed the administrative work because he could see the results of his efforts almost immediately, but he found college with its rote requirements tedious. He complained frequently to Kellen, but his brother refused to change the agreement—no school, no job. So Mickey soldiered on to get his associate's degree.

As Kellen's company grew, he opened a small operation in Miami and asked Mickey to move there and run it, but with the same condition: He would continue his college education. Kellen worried that when presented with freedom and money, Mickey might squander it, as he had done in the past. Mickey agreed to the deal. He opened up the new facility and staffed it with an able crew. When Kellen visited the site, he was surprised not so much by the excellent job his little brother could do but by his changed nature. Mickey was doggedly focused and driven to accomplishment.

Taking double the recommended course load, Mickey graduated in one year with his bachelor's degree, and then continued on to get his MBA without telling his brother what he was doing. Meanwhile, the business continued to grow. Mickey took on responsibilities well beyond the scope of his job. In time, he helped engineer a major acquisition for what was now the family business.

What Kellen had done was to provide the colors Mickey was lacking. He knew his brother needed to honor commitments and follow through on what was expected of him—red traits—but he also had such strong family feeling for Mickey, and knew him so well, that he could enforce these red lessons in a supportive, "yellow" way. As Mickey came out of the negative zone, he began to experience success, and he was willing to give up his old, extreme approach to inventing his life. He added some red, yellow, and blue to his all-green palette. Mickey had escaped the negative zone in what may be the only way: He let in other people to tell him what he didn't want to hear and to work on the sides of the problem he hadn't wanted to acknowledge.

In other words, we are back to the importance of lighting your fires where the sparks of diversity fly—not just when you're launching a new innovation, but throughout. The more you have a characteristic approach, the more important it is that you consult and embrace the approaches of the opposite type. You have to know where to find them, and to build relationships with people you can trust because you're going to need to listen to them.

When it comes to success at innovation, diversity is the great card. I've built my business on green and blue, but my most trusted mentor is a former CEO, a brilliant Control who also has some Compete. He doesn't tell me the things I want to hear, but he tells me what I need to hear. My other important mentor is a yellow who is highly sensitive to the differences between communities and the harm that can be done when you don't speak their language. He'll tell me: You shouldn't have spoken that way, it came off harsh. Do I like to hear that? No. But I'm grateful for the ways my mentors keep me out of the negative zone. Whenever I'm starting a new project, I'll gather those people for lunch and say, Here's what I'm planning. Tell me what you think.

It's not only people who can slip into the negative zone. The same happens to organizations and, sometimes, entire countries. Part of watching the weather successfully is to be on the lookout for storms of the negative so you can take action, take shelter, or take the next ride out of town.

match your approach to your goal

When an entire organization is in the negative zone, there is often very little any one individual can do about it. That was the experience of my friend Liz. One of seven children from a blue-collar family in an industrial downriver neighborhood, she managed to make enough money working as a secretary for a cement company to attend a nearby community college. There, she fell in love with writing. Upon graduation she moved to Cleveland to work as a copywriter for a financial institution, where her combination of creativity, drive, and practical understanding of ordinary bank customers' lives got recognized. She moved up the ranks, eventually becoming senior vice president of marketing. Senior management never warmed to her personally, and in fact she often felt uncomfortable and isolated. Nevertheless, she crafted ingenious and successful marketing campaigns.

Because of her position in the company, she sat in on meetings where she could see that the bank was in trouble. She was smart enough to understand the new forms of loans they were offering, in which the recipients paid only interest for the first few years, then saw their payments go up dramatically. She knew from experience that the working people who were taking these loans were not going to see dramatic increases in income: When their payments ballooned, they would be hard pressed to meet them. She spoke up, making her usual insightful and compelling case: The bank needed to rethink its decision to offer these crazy loans to this target group. She was told, essentially, to sit down and shut up. The bank was in a breakneck race for market share with other banks who were also offering these extremely easy loans, and senior management didn't want anything slowing the company down.

Defaults increased, and in a few years the bank became insolvent. Most of senior management was fired—though, amazingly, not the CEO who had green-lighted the imprudent loans. He called Liz to his office, and she went to the meeting excited, expecting a promotion. He told her she was a poor team player and gave her an hour to collect her things. Liz was stunned. She had never imagined that her good counsel and being helpful would result in being fired. But we've all seen this happen—the person who is right and virtuous, the person who didn't go along, gets hung out to dry.

When she reflected on it, she acknowledged she had never felt comfortable with senior management; they had never shown any interest in her intelligence or her insights, only in her ability to sell, sell, sell. Management had been in the negative zone of "blue" for a long time, and it only valued her for her ability to help them compete. The organization could not tolerate even a small amount of a Collaborate approach, not even when she was right, not even when the entire company was at risk. There was nothing for her to do but move on, and to look in the future for the warning signs of the negative zone when she was ready to join other organizations.

If one thing unites these two dangers on the path to innovation— failing to empty the bag and falling into the negative zone—it's that in both cases we stop being mindful of whether our approach matches our goals. Success at innovation requires that we keep checking in: What does this situation require of us now? Have we considered all four colors? Have we stacked all three nesting dolls? What parts of our approach no longer justify the effort to carry them around?

It would be far simpler if there was a simple success checklist that everyone could follow, but when it comes to innovation, one size can never fit all. The only checklist that actually works is the one that you create based on your own prismatic thinking.

step III

RUN YOUR EXPERIMENTS

In theory, there is no difference between theory and practice.
In practice, there is.
—Yogi Berra

In the 1990s, when the utilities were deregulated, engineers at power companies were suddenly free to innovate in new ways. After decades of taking a Control approach, following strict federal regulations that only permitted them to make small changes in how the business was run, they could now look for their own new opportunities for growth and innovation. The possibilities were wide open: They were free to generate power in new ways, develop remote sensing technologies to anticipate equipment failure, and create sophisticated algorithms to predict energy spot trading. I was asked to work with one of these large power companies, and I began by helping my new client identify an elite team of young engineers to develop new projects. We thought that the sky was the limit.

Unfortunately, we soon discovered that although our elite team was talented and well trained, excited by their new freedoms, and soon developing more creative and competitive ideas, they got nowhere when it came to setting practical targets to implement those ideas. Apparently they'd never had a chance to innovate beyond their usual one way. Every time a new pilot project didn't work as planned, the team got knotted up and angry—emphasizing small failures, assigning blame, turning against one another, and complaining that their ideas were stupid to begin with. Soon some wanted off the team entirely.

Working with the engineers made me think of twin sisters, Dale and Carla. They were both smart, hardworking gals, successful in their jobs and interested in staying healthy. They also shared a biological tendency to put on weight, even when they were getting regular exercise. They had often talked about this personal challenge, and over the years they had undertaken many of the same strategies—diets, exercise programs—but without getting lasting results.

At one point, Dale, the older twin, decided on what she called a foolproof method: She would double the number of hours she went to the gym each week, from two to four, keeping the length of each workout constant, and at the same time she would adopt the rule that she could eat nothing after four in the afternoon except salad. In this way, she planned to increase the number of calories she burned while decreasing the calories she took in. It was, she said, a foolproof method. Carla agreed to keep her company in this rigorous Control approach to losing weight.

Dale had set clear, ambitious targets, and for nearly two weeks she met them. The third week, however, she faltered. She was just so sick of greens. She missed her targets repeatedly, and she was very hard on herself. She felt that all was lost. Like the engineers I described, she assigned blame, cast doubt on the entire project, and wanted to give up. Within a month, her attempt at personal innovation was nothing more than a humiliating memory. What had gone wrong?

Dale's attempts broke down when she tried to turn her general approach into a specific method. The focus of Step III is to avoid this pitfall. The most important rule is to proceed not by betting everything on one make-or-break method, as Dale did, but by experimenting with a range of possibilities in order to learn which ones move you closer to where you want to be. Like a baseball manager, you will learn not to ask for a home run every time your players are at bat. Instead, you'll learn to play "small ball": If you can get one batter to first base, advance that player with a sacrifice bunt; now you have a runner on second who might score on a well-hit single.

The questions to explore in Step III are:

- What experiments could I run? How might I reach short-term targets that would move me closer to my goal?
- Who knows what I need to know to run those experiments? Who could assist me in carrying them out?
- Can I find more than one way to try to reach each target?
- After I run my experiments, what can I learn from the results to make me wiser next time?

Here in Step III, you will find new and powerful ways to answer these questions. The first several chapters in Step III help you to create and select the best "experiments" for your situation and goals. Often those experiments will show that you lack expertise to succeed, so the next few chapters show you how to acquire the practical knowledge—including the real-life experience and street smarts—to reach your goals. Through your experiments, you will discover areas where you can't do it all yourself. I'll show you how to make use of the community around you to find the partners who can make your experiments more successful, whether those others share your specific goals or not. Finally, I'll explain how to review each attempt you make in order to learn the most you can about what will work best for you as you prepare your next set of attempts.

Depending on what exactly you're trying to make new in your life, you won't always answer these questions in the same order. Sometimes an experiment has to fail before you realize that you need a partner or an ally to make it succeed; other times, you won't know what experiment would be worth trying until you get some good advice. So the chapters in Step III are not intended as a checklist that must be performed in a precise order; instead, my goals are to help you recognize each need as it arises and to give you the tools to handle each one.

There are four key steps that you need:

1. Set high-quality targets—chapter 18.
2. Enlist deep and diverse domain expertise—chapter 19.
3. Take multiple shots on goal—chapter 22.
4. Learn from experience and experiments—chapter 28.

In the next few chapters, I will explain how each of these steps will help you innovate your life.

chapter fifteen

COMMIT TO EXPERIMENT

Dale's sister, Carla, also tried the strict exercise and diet regimen her older sister had devised, but she didn't even last a week. However, she had a different attitude than Dale about setting targets and getting results. Though she was disappointed that her sister's method wasn't a miracle cure, she viewed it as one experiment out of many; rather than berating herself, she was more reflective about the experience. Like a scientist, she made observations about what she had tried and what results she had gotten.

How did Carla feel eating only salads after four? Eating a lot of lettuce for dinner, she found, left her feeling so unsatisfied that she almost always ate other things later on in the evening, things that she hadn't meant to eat. Dale's approach, which had seemed so logical, actually made it harder, not easier, for Carla to eat fewer calories. Similarly, going to the gym more made her realize something she had never quite put into words before: She didn't like gyms. They were noisy and lonely, she felt, and she didn't like being watched by strangers while she sweated and strained on some machine. It didn't matter if she signed up for classes or hired a trainer. She still found reasons not to go to the gym. Four times a week became two became one.

When Carla thought about it, she realized that when she wasn't at work, she didn't want to be feeling alone at a gym. She wanted to be with her friends somewhere they could hear each other talk. One day she heard from a former school friend that there was a group that met two or three times a week at lunch to go walking in the mall. She started walking with them, often spending her full lunch hour on the move, with just a quick stop at a convenient and delicious yogurt place they showed her on the way back to the office. Now she was getting regular exercise and eating healthier, and it didn't feel bad to her at all.

small discoveries, big changes

Experimenting more with healthy food other than salad, Carla found that snacking on peanuts during the late afternoon satisfied her, and that she could eat a lot of peanuts and still not gain weight. Often she got through the afternoon snacking in that way, and then had a small portion of "real food" for dinner.

Over the years, the results the two sisters saw couldn't have been more different. Self-critical Dale became obese, meaning that her extra weight threatened her health. Carla's weight varied, but she kept it within a healthy range. The difference was that Dale expected innovation to move in a short, straight line, the shortest possible distance from problem to solution. Like the engineers at the power company, she formulated a method, made an attempt, failed, and then placed blame and quit. Carla, though, thought of innovation more like a scientific journey with many steps, and she was willing to experiment and reflect on her results. Carla asked herself what my engineers were forgetting to ask: What happened here? How do we get smarter from it? What simple rules can we divine? She understood that she might not have solved the whole exercise-and-diet problem this time around but that each attempt was an experiment, and experiments are chances to learn. An experiment that succeeds tells you something. An experiment that fails tells you something else.

But they are both good experiments because they bring new information—discoveries—and sometimes a small discovery, even peanuts, can be important. What matters is not that you innovate perfectly the first time you try, but that you commit to experiment and learn from your results.

Don't you ever move from "experiments" to the "real thing"? In innovation terms, no. Innovators think of every action as an experiment. The *Apollo 11* mission, which achieved the nation's goal of landing on the moon, was still an experiment: It provided crucial data for the later moon missions, the space shuttle program, and all of NASA's ongoing work. The fact that it was a historic success means that it was a great experiment, but to an innovator it was just as important as a chance to learn for the future.

chapter sixteen

HEDGE NOW, OPTIMIZE LATER

After he lost his job, my colleague Kenji came to me for advice. He'd had success as a marketer for a large energy company, showing a real gift for segmenting the market and creating processes and brand maps to help his company reach its goals. However, despite his skills and past successes, in the recession his company scaled back and he lost his job.

As we talked about his options, I could tell he'd already given good thought to innovating in his professional life. He was comfortable with a Compete approach, and he thrived on reaching sales goals in a pressured atmosphere. Through experience he knew that these were qualities that could benefit the companies he worked for—he was a blue who knew his niche.

Kenji had also creativized well. As a Japanese American, he had ties to Japan and a lasting interest in Far Eastern countries and their growing energy needs. This was an area where he hoped to ride what moved. Among his friends from business school, he kept in touch with a group that was especially interested in East Asian markets, and they met to compare notes and help each other spot opportunities—he was beginning to light his fire where sparks fly. Already, in fact, he had been offered several small consulting gigs, though none was the job he was looking for. He told me his plan was to turn them all down and give his full attention to finding the job he thought would match his abilities and situation best: a small, entrepreneurial start-up in the field of energy. Could I help him design some "experiments" that would help him hit that target?

I told him, yes, I could do that, but before he experimented with ways to reach one target, he should experiment with a wider *range* of targets. It was not yet time to optimize—to give everything he'd got to reach any one type of target, such as energy start-ups. At the beginning of innovating is the time to hedge your bets. Start thinking of your life the way an investor thinks of a portfolio. Broaden your possibilities. Place several different bets, and don't hesitate to place a few long shots. Some will fail, but you only need one big success—one great job offer—to make the whole series of experiments worthwhile.

To help Kenji start, I suggested he could broaden his definition of the kind of job that matched his skills and experience. Energy is a regulated field with large production, so as I saw it, his skills would also apply in any field with the same general attribute: not just energy, but also pharmaceuticals (highly regulated), aerospace (also regulated, also with a large scale and many moving parts), even consumer electronics. And why limit yourself to start-ups? I asked him. You've already run a major marketing campaign; that's much bigger than anything a start-up would need you to do. In these ways I helped him to hedge his bets about which industry might suit him. Now he had not one but four industries where he might possibly reach his goal—four times the chances to succeed.

be a target detective

When it comes to setting targets, we are all detectives. We are gathering clues and trying to solve a complex puzzle. A terrible detective will learn of a crime and then arrest whomever is nearby. On the other hand, the best detectives allow their thinking to "diverge," casting as wide a net as possible to find as many clues and witnesses as they can. Based on what is learned from this information-gathering and thought-expanding work, a good detective converges on a new, narrower target—suspects—but then within that narrower category, the detective diverges again, casting an equally wide net for suspects. Only then does he or she converge on the few most likely suspects. Then, the best detective casts the wide net for ideas about where the suspects might be located. This alternating movement, from diverging to converging, from hedging your bets to optimizing for your most desirable outcomes, helps great detectives and great innovators of every kind to deal with the most frustrating aspect of opportunity: Most opportunities only offer part of what we want. A job may be what you want to do, but not at the level of compensation you want to make. It may be the right work at the right pay, but offer no promise of future advancement. It may satisfy you in all three categories, but require you to live in the wrong place, or work unaccustomed hours, or include a dozen other undesired complications. But even though opportunities rarely come in perfect form, that's not necessarily a reason to reject them.

First consider whether you could treat each opportunity as an "investment" in your overall innovation "portfolio." Just as investors mix different kinds of investments, diversifying their portfolios because they don't know which kinds of investments will succeed when, look for the chance to try several approaches at once or to take on several part-time projects. That way, even if you are wrong about some, there are others that can still succeed—perhaps in ways that surprise you. As a rule, whenever you have a goal, you have the greatest chance of success if you are *unyielding about where you want to go, but flexible about how you get there, especially as new information emerges.*

Back in Step I, I said that there is no data about the future. Hedging them first and optimizing them later is a powerful way to develop targets in part because it works without any special knowledge of the future: Instead of trying to be a brilliant predictor of which approaches will succeed and which will fail, you try them all and let the results of your experiments make your decisions for you. In this way, a committed experimenter often winds up more successful than a brilliant analyst.

Sometimes this approach is enough to carry a person from a very unpromising beginning all the way through a satisfying life. Consider Jack, a young man who never did anything according to plan. Growing up in a factory town in the middle of Wisconsin dairy country, he was also musically talented: He played guitar in a band and liked to perform in musicals at the local church theater. Still, it was widely assumed that he would go to work on the assembly line or be a manager at the local burger joint, where he frequently hung out. So it was a surprise to the entire school community when he was called to the guidance counselor's office. Always a mediocre student, the clown at the back of the class, Jack had scored in the top 1 percent of all Wisconsin high school graduates on a college admissions test. After double-checking to make sure it wasn't a mistake or an act of cheating, the counselor suggested that Jack enroll in the regional campus of the state university. Jack defiantly announced that he planned to go to Broadway to be an actor, a director, and a playwright. However, at the urging of his older brother, Jack visited the university, which had a thriving theater program. The school offered to waive his tuition because of his test scores. He enrolled the following semester.

Jack joined the oratorical society, majored in film and theater, played guitar in folk bistros in Chicago on the weekends, and graduated a year early with honors. His study habits were bizarre: He made giant storyboards of complex subjects and how they interrelated, and his class presentations were usually deemed "unusual." With degree in hand and finally ready to make the move to New York, Jack was offered a scholarship to attend graduate school and teach public speaking at a top university. Jack went on to become an influential professor of rhetoric. At his twenty-fifth high school reunion, a classmate remarked that she always thought he would go on to be a performer. Jack thought about it and realized a performer was exactly what he had become. But for him, experience had refined his targets as he grew. His inexperienced vision of a life in theater had grown into a passion for teaching; the gifts that had informed the music he wrote were also well suited to writing academic papers. He found his Broadway in the ivory tower. Jack had innovated a far more successful and satisfying life than anyone had ever reasonably imagined for him—and, in fact, a more satisfying life than he could have described when he first began expressing his goals. He had done it by remaining true to his natural approach and talents, but hedging about his specific targets until he discovered the goals that could satisfy him.

chapter seventeen

DECONSTRUCT TO RECONSTRUCT

It's one thing to say you need to experiment, but where to begin? Often as you begin Step III, it can seem like you have nothing to work with. Yet you always do—you have whatever it is that isn't working. You have the broken thing that inspired you to innovate in the first place.

In the developing world, you can find many mechanics who can build a new car out of the parts of a broken-down old car. They make lots of jokes at the West's expense, because we throw away so much that still works. I'm saying that we can take the same recycler's approach to the parts of our lives that need to be renewed. Start with the thing or the situation that needs innovating. Take it apart; break it into its component pieces. Then once you've deconstructed it, look at the pieces and consider how you could use them in new ways.

Lately I've been watching journalist friends do this. Journalism is a field that's collapsed. Many of the newspapers and magazines where journalists made their careers are gone, and many that remain (whether traditional or online) pay little or nothing. Some longtime reporters have walked away, feeling that there is nothing left. But others have deconstructed their old approach in order to find material to put something new together.

The old career model for journalists was straightforward, with three key parts: (a) develop an understanding of your "beat"; (b) write accurate, insightful articles about it; and (c) get paid for those articles by the publication that distributes your stories to an audience. Now, as many of the established publications can no longer afford the old arrangement, the journalists who are surviving are breaking the old three-step model down into its parts and getting creative with each part. Some still know their "beat," but they're doing their research and analysis for think tanks and corporations that need to have an up-to-the-minute understanding of a given industry or part of the world: They're still doing "journalist thinking," but they're selling their thinking to specialized readers. Others still write articles in the usual way, but they don't have newspapers or magazines to publish them, so they blog and tweet, comment on radio or television news, and create their own websites. Some attract their own subscribers and advertisers. Instead of writing for a publication, they use the Internet to become their own publication. The best at this have found that the top publications come to them and ask to link the newspaper's website to their own—now, instead of a journalist applying for a job at *The New York Times* to share in its appeal, *The New York Times* instead seeks to stay relevant by linking to popular writers' blogs. All this doesn't mean the problems of journalists are solved, but some of these writers are taking the first step in launching the cycle of innovation: They have begun to deconstruct in order to reconstruct.

Take a mental inventory of the part of your life that needs to be made new and improved. What in it seems old and defective? Begin to see this part of your life with a recycler's eyes. What are the parts—good or bad? What could be hammered into something new? What skills, what relationships, what experiences can you bring forward into your new situation? Make a list of everything that has stopped working. Now consider that these may be the pieces of the new vehicle you've been waiting for. Stop seeing a junkyard and start seeing a storehouse.

chapter eighteen

SET HIGH-QUALITY TARGETS

Setting targets tends to bring out the macho in all of us. I've seen many promising individuals become so stuck in their grand personal visions that they set pie-in-the-sky targets they can never reach: quit smoking forever in a week, lose twenty-five pounds next month, multiply earnings tenfold next year—and in their spare time, boil the ocean to extract gold. People who espouse big talk like "Go big or go home" usually wind up doing the latter. So what makes a great target?

Even if you are committed to experimenting—willing to hedge before you optimize and ready to break apart what doesn't work to find the pieces you can still use—it can be hard to be sure you are setting good targets. How can you be sure that you're not just chasing illusions, or, on the other side, holding yourself back by not asking enough?

High-quality targets are ones that can pass these three tests:

1. *Is my target specific?* Not "I will be rich," but rather, "In five years I'll have paid off my house, with enough extra to cover two yearly vacations." High-quality targets are things you can measure in ways everyone would agree on—not "I will work more on my sculptures this summer," but "I will complete ten models in clay and

three finished castings in bronze by Labor Day." High-quality targets have end dates. They are things you can be certain about. They are brief. (The warning sign of a failed target: The description rambles. You don't know what you're trying to hit, so it's impossible to succeed.) Jack's wish to "make it on Broadway" was not a specific target; it was a long, winding road: When would he have counted himself as having "made it"? When he got a role in a Broadway show? Any role? What would happen if that show closed?

2. *Is my target feasible?* A high-quality target is something that can be done and, more important, something you or your organization can do. The workout and diet targets that sisters Dale and Carla set were specific and worthwhile, but their experiments quickly showed that they weren't humanly possible, at least not for those two human beings. Carla's later success came because of her willingness and her ability to revise her targets based on her failed experiments, until she found targets that were not just specific but also feasible for her.

3. *Is my target a "wow"?* We hit the targets that move us. If a target doesn't have the subjective, personal feeling of "wow," it's not an innovation target, it's just an ordinary goal, unlikely to promise the deep personal satisfaction that motivates us best. And what makes a "wow" varies with our preferred approaches to innovation:

- For a yellow, who favors a Collaborate approach, a wow target is a chance to make productive harmony, with everyone pulling together to succeed.
- For a green, who favors a Create approach, a wow is an "Everest goal," something no one has done before, at least not in the way that this particular innovator wants to do it.
- For a blue, who favors a Compete approach, the target must be a quantitative goal on a dramatic timetable: I will hit my numbers in six months.
- For a red, who favors a Control approach, the target must

be a solution that works like a key: Every time you turn it, the lock opens. That consistency or process means that success in reaching your target will raise your status: You will be known as the key maker.

what if you're not sure?

What if you're not certain you have picked the right targets? What if you're not sure that you know what you want? *Continue with the process.* Make target setting your first target for now. Set some possible targets and try them out, following the process I'm describing here in Step III. This is why applicants to college and graduate schools are always urged to visit first, if they can. Once you see a few schools, you'll discover many aspects of what matters to you based on the experiences you have during the visit. There is no effective substitute for walking around a place, talking to people, and observing how they go about their days.

In the same way, if you're uncertain about your targets for any innovation, then explore the possible targets by trying them out. What you want will emerge and change over time as you have more experiences. So set the highest-quality targets that you can, coming as close as you can to the guidelines I've listed—even if that isn't all that close—and trust that as you make your way through the cycles of innovation, the big existential questions (What do I really want? Who am I?) will take care of themselves.

My model here is venture capital firms. Imagine a firm that wants to invest in the next big drug for a given disease. Their goal is clear: to fund development of a new drug and profit from its sales. But out of all the researchers all over the world, which ones should they fund? Which targets are worthwhile?

Let's imagine that a venture capitalist (VC) assigned to this project does some research and discovers, say, that there are twelve promising approaches being developed to combat one specific illness.

Say the firm has a maximum of thirty million dollars for this investment. Which of the twelve approaches should the company fund? Many people who don't do this for a living would probably try to pick two or three promising research groups and give them a lot of support. But at this stage a VC will give all twelve promising drug development firms some money. This is known as the angel phase. Perhaps the firm gives each one a million dollars, and then watches to see which ones make progress.

Very often the one that looked best at the start won't test very well. More than half will fail quickly, but perhaps out of twelve there will be five that still seem like they could succeed. Now the VC sells off what didn't work, takes the loss, and focuses on the remaining areas of promise. The firm might give each of the remaining ones another two million dollars. (This is known as the mezzanine phase.) Out of those five, four will probably fail, but one might get very close to success.

Now, from one point of view, the VC firm has now wasted a huge amount of money on ventures that failed. But that's missing the point. It's true that they have spent twenty-two million dollars with no results. But with that money they have learned how to invest brilliantly—and the one brilliant investment can make the entire expenditure worthwhile. So now the VC gives eight million dollars— most of its remaining budget—to the organization that's on the brink of success, to do everything they can to help that organization take the last, necessary steps.

Of course, I realize you probably don't have a spare thirty million. But in any situation where you have to pick targets, the best approach will be to pick a larger number of targets and spend some of what you've got—money, time, resources, and caring—to try each one out. Want to find a new romance? You might start by going on a lot of first dates.

Or say you've got a two-week vacation coming up. You're not going to travel, you're going to stay at home and do things you never get to do otherwise. But now that you have some time, what's the best way to use it?

Let's say you've daydreamed about moving up to the next level of yoga classes, trying mountain biking (you've had a bike for years but you've barely used it), returning to voice lessons, going swimming, seeing some old friends, and reading in your favorite bookstore café. There are a lot of people who might get excited at the beginning of the vacation and make an impulsive commitment—plunking down the money for two weeks of intensive yoga classes, say. But you'd be wiser to "fund" each of your options a little bit. In the first weekend of your vacation, take a yoga class and a voice lesson. Get out the bike and see how it feels. Go for a swim. Find friends to do some of these things with you. Spend some time alone at your favorite bookstore café. That way, you won't commit a lot of time and money to something that turns out not to work for you. And you won't come to find that on the last night, when you finally make it to the café with a book, you wish you'd been making time to read every day.

Like a venture capitalist, you should be willing to put in some effort just to find out which targets are worthwhile and which aren't—not by guessing, but by giving each one a practical chance. Most people pick too few targets, invest too much too soon, and lose it all because they never had the right "target" to begin with. This even happens among the pros at the Innovatrium, my innovation lab. There are always people who are convinced they know from the start which approach we're testing with a client is going to be effective. Despite the fact that they work in an innovation business, they're still almost always wrong. We have to be willing to start with the best targets we can find, for now, and trust to the larger process of innovation to sort them out.

chapter nineteen

———

ENLIST DEEP AND DIVERSE
DOMAIN EXPERTISE

In a famous Monty Python skit, a timid accountant named Mr. Anchovy enters a career placement office to talk about changing careers. He explains to the job counselor that what he really wants is to be a lion tamer. Puzzled, the counselor asks about Mr. Anchovy's experience with lion taming. The fearful man replies that he has seen lions at the zoo. He has even purchased a pith helmet, he says, as part of his future lion tamer's outfit. Finally, the counselor shows him a film of a menacing lion leaping at its prey with fangs and claws bared. Mr. Anchovy shrieks in terror and begins to babble about a possible career in banking.

Easy as it is to laugh at Mr. Anchovy, the fact is that all of us sometimes try to build innovations in our lives without laying a solid foundation of knowledge or expertise. Real estate agents confirm year after year that retirees are one of the most transient groups in any community, moving to a new home in another part of the country or the world—and then moving again when their new lives fail to live up to their hopes. Despite their life experience and wisdom (they know themselves well, they have picked out places to live before, and they are experienced with the human condition), retirees are often likely to make some of the worst decisions about where to move. What goes wrong? In making their decisions, they lack expertise in the one area that, to them, matters most: Often they know almost nothing about what it will be like to *live as retirees* in the new place. They trust their "best places to live" guides, their friends' choices, and their daydreams, but what they need is practical expertise about their own personal targets: a retirement that will satisfy them. Like poor Mr. Anchovy, they have set targets without gathering any practical knowledge.

I think of those retirees when I hear people say, as they often do, that the guys who founded Google, reinventing the way all of us find the information we need, were amateurs. They were just smart young guys with computers, the story goes—the new self-made men, proof that with a laptop, creativity, and grit, you can do anything. I have great respect for what Google has built, but when I hear that explanation of their success at reaching their targets, I have to laugh. The founders of Google were PhD students in information technology at Stanford. They studied with some of the best minds in their field. Before their "overnight success," they put in years of serious—and, in their case, very traditional—work. It reminds me of what Picasso once told a journalist who was surprised at how fast he painted: "It took me twenty years to learn to paint this fast."

In order to reinvent anything, whether it's the rules for hosting your book group or the future of information technology, you have to make sure you have good information. After you set targets but before you attempt to reach them, you will probably need to seek out some expertise. That might sound obvious, but it is exactly when you are innovating—doing something you haven't done before in a way you haven't done it—that you may fail to realize you've wandered into unfamiliar territory where your old understanding is no longer enough. That's how retirees go wrong picking new places to live.

When you find a lack in your understanding or your skills, as everyone does sometimes, what matters is that you seek help from true experts, what we call in business those with "deep and diverse domain expertise." Those are people who, within their domain, are the experts whose knowledge goes both deep and wide. A master plumber has seen pretty much everything that can go wrong with pipes and fixtures, and can fix them all. A parent who's seen a kid through school knows a great deal about what can go wrong and right in a family. That's deep and diverse domain expertise.

Sometimes, the expert you need may be you. If you are a retiree considering moving to a warmer climate, for example, you can read and discuss all you like, but if what you want to know is whether you can make a life for yourself in a new place, the only person who can tell you that is you—after you've been there. So before you commit to a new home, or any other long-term commitment, visit for a season or for as long as you can. Ideally, take an extended visit in more than one possible location, so you have a basis for comparison. Become the expert you need in what your next phase of life would be like. That's the knowledge that will let you move to a new place with confidence.

Often, however, you will need to consult someone else. I wonder whether we Americans have a particular difficulty in seeking out this kind of expertise. Like the Typical Man who will never ask for directions, many Americans often think we can do it all. Many of us were told when we were young that we could be anything we wanted to be. We were raised on the mantra, "You can do it!" But I'm sorry to tell you, if you're an adult reading this book, that's simply not true anymore. There are all sorts of abilities that require more practice and study than you will ever put in again, so even though you once had the potential to be a tax attorney or a master plumber or a Web designer, most of those chances are gone now. You need to recognize the limits of your own expertise and accept that others have put in the time and effort to build knowledge and skills you will never have. I know far too many business school professors who manage their own investments—terribly. They are experts in their fields but they are not experts in personal finance, and it costs them. When it comes to innovation, we are all would-be lion tamers, just one thoughtless "You can do it!" away from being consumed by ravenous lions, or at least by our own hungry fantasies. Be clear about where your domain expertise ends.

What that means, practically, is that after you set your goals but before you try to reach them, you need to spend an hour of your time and money with a person who has studied deeply the things you need to understand. The Internet is not enough. The library is not enough. Pick up the phone. Stop by the office of a fellow human being. You are there to get more than facts. Let your experts hear what you want to do and let them give you the benefit of their experience and perspective: how your specific "experiment" looks to them.

"Expert" is of course a relative term—the person you need is not necessarily the one with the most letters after his or her name. If you're a housewife with a gift for reviving plants that other people would throw in the trash, and you think you might like to start blogging about your approach to plant care but have no idea how to create and manage a blog, the sixteen-year-old across the street who lives for her Tumblr blog may be just the expert you need. And it may be that barter or even friendship, rather than money, will get you the expertise you need. Just make sure you talk with real experts.

chapter twenty

———

APPRENTICE THE SORCERER

I often advise MBAs before they graduate: Don't worry about which company you will work for when you finish school. Focus on whose apprentice you can be once you're there. Find a person who can do the things you want to do—there is no substitute for getting close enough to see exactly how it's done. This is as essential to career development as it is to raising resourceful kids. We learn the methods of the people we observe up close. And that is more valuable than any company's name on your résumé.

Mickey Mouse seemed to understand this in Walt Disney's "The Sorcerer's Apprentice," when he stole the pointed blue cap of Yen Sid, the magician who employed him to sweep up, and tried to do the sorcerer's magic for himself. As the spells got beyond his control, Mickey quickly awakened to the reality that he was beyond his depth and in real peril. Just in time, the grouchy magician reappeared to undo the foolish spell of the amateur and to restore calm to the situation. He scolded Mickey to get back to work carrying water and walloped him with a broom, knowing that his young apprentice, while lacking in skill, had demonstrated the desire and sacred will to learn the craft.

As you consider the kind and amount of expertise you need in order to run your experiments, you may come to realize that the targets you have set require more than an hour or two of expert advice. Like Dan, who reimagined karate for his young American students by studying child psychology, you may discover that what you need is not just advice but ongoing coaching in an approach that is new to you. To get it, try finding a sorcerer—someone who can do what you want to do so easily that it seems like magic—and becoming his or her apprentice. Whether you want to learn to play chess, get back to dating after many years, or take advantage of new technologies that for you, right now, are so foreign they might as well be magic, consider finding a master practitioner. The role of that master practitioner is not to be a know-it-all or to protect you from failure, but rather to provide you with opportunities to make attempts, get into trouble, and give you guidance when you request it. That way, you can learn your own lessons, but faster.

what's in it for the sorcerer?

Why would anyone take you on as an apprentice? To begin with, most people like to share their gifts. It is gratifying to have an interested and appreciative companion who wants to learn what you can do. When people ask me if I'll mentor them as innovators, I often find that if they make it easy for me and we're on the same path, I'm happy to do it. In addition, apprentices may do things that the master practitioner needs done, such as sweeping up, as Mickey Mouse does for Yen Sid. If you are willing to be helpful in the ways that you can, it can make all the difference. In my neighborhood, I've been observing a boy in his teens who follows a contractor around: The young man carries cement blocks for the older man and helps him move generators, and in return the older man shows the boy the tricks of the trade.

In the same way, when the Scottish inventor James Watt first came to London in the 1700s, he apprenticed himself to a brass smith. Watt wanted to build machines, and he had a gift: In time, he would revolutionize the steam engine, invent the concept of horse-power, help kick the industrial revolution into high gear, and have the unit of power measurement—the "watt"—named after him. But before he could do all that, he was an apprentice. He learned how to make high-quality brass machinery—very useful if you wanted to design steam engines in the eighteenth century—and he provided manpower and problem-solving for the smith. No doubt there were days he felt impatient, knowing that his head was full of inventions his "master" might never understand. But in the end, the arrangement benefited both. To put it in more modern terms: Sometimes you must be willing to be the one who stands and asks, "Would you like fries with that?"

chapter twenty-one

MASTER SODOTO

When the great mountain climber Edmund Hillary set his sights on the summit of Mount Everest, he knew his own experience and knowledge as a climber would not be enough to reach his goal. He also knew that there was no expert who could explain how to do what he wanted to do, and no sorcerer to take him on as an apprentice, because no one else had ever reached the summit before. What choices remained?

He began to ask a student's questions: Who has been close to the summit? Could I learn from him? He teamed up with Tenzing Norgay, who had taken part in earlier attempts to reach the summit over two decades. In one of their early climbing outings together, Hillary fell into a crevasse, but as he fell, Tenzing saved his life by securing his rope with an ice ax. From then on, Hillary trusted his expertise and selected him as his climbing partner.

Hillary and Tenzing learned from each other while the two made further attempts. When they reached the summit, they refused for a long time to say who got there first, insisting that they had reached it as a team. Hillary later taught the methods he had watched and practiced with Tenzing. Norgay's son, Peter, was one of his students and eventually reached the summit as well.

These mountain climbers were using an approach like the one at the heart of every traditional culture of learning, whether the Japanese sensei and student or the Indian guru and disciple. It's also at the heart of modern medical teaching, in which students follow established doctors on their rounds, perform procedures under supervision, and then in turn are observed and teach others. You find a similar approach in the teaching of classical music: first-year Juilliard students attend numerous musical performances and receive intense classroom instruction. With each of the succeeding years, the emphasis shifts to performance in multiple ensembles and genres. The instruction becomes increasingly experiential, with personalized coaching to hone technique. Finally, upperclassmen are expected to assist their junior colleagues in developing their abilities.

But while this method for developing deep expertise is associated with many established organizations, the method doesn't require them. What is necessary is to recognize that while talent and practice are enough to develop basic competency, they are insufficient to master it. The deepest knowledge and most reliable mastery come when you pursue them in three ways at once: (a) seeing it done, (b) trying it for yourself, and (c) teaching it to others. At the Innovatrium, my innovation lab, we use a term common to artisans, SODOTO: See One, Do One, Teach One.

Each of these three approaches to learning adds deeper understanding of both the intricacies of theory and the surprises of actual practice. "Seeing one" provides practical perspective that doing alone can't offer. Our would-be lion tamer was amusing in part because he had apparently never seen so much as an image of a lion on the attack. Of course, an actual lion tamer would want to spend thousands of hours watching lions and lion tamers, just as a serious athlete will watch video footage of games and even practice sessions to observe every detail of the activity on the field. The risk of not first "seeing one" can be significant: Someone who enrolls in nursing school only to discover that the sight of blood makes him faint has learned too late that he must find another way to express his desire to care for others.

After "seeing one" comes "doing one," which makes practical the parts of expertise that can't be seen. Doing takes what is only abstract and vague when we're reading and makes it concrete. When information can be interpreted and absorbed through activity, a higher level of learning occurs. Ideas converge with actions, and direct feedback from experience (including the experience of supervision) alerts us to what is working and what isn't. As John Dewey, the founder of the progressive education movement, put it, we "learn by doing," not least because "failure is instructive."

"Teaching one" requires that the teacher really know his or her stuff. A group of serious students with their own distinctive questions and confusions can test a teacher's knowledge in ways no practical experience ever can. Teaching also forces the practitioner to put into words the new ideas and new ways of doing things that he or she may have developed but never explained—often innovators don't know exactly what they have innovated, or how to do it again—until an eager student pushes them to render the formula in words. Like the cook in a family who knows all the old family favorites but measures by eye and doesn't actually know the formal recipe, teachers of all kinds discover what they know in part by putting it into words for an eager student.

Practicing SODOTO is the best guarantee that you will develop deep and diverse enough expertise to run worthwhile experiments and ultimately make your innovations succeed. That's why the approach is formalized in institutions across so many cultures. But while the institutions make it easier to get ample opportunity to see, do, and teach, these institutions are not necessary. Not every great musician goes to Juilliard. If you find that you lack the expertise you need to attempt to reach the targets you have set for yourself, and there is no expert sorcerer who will take you on for a season (or even for an hour), you can still build the expertise you need if you look for opportunities to see, to do, and to teach.

Pete has never kept complete or organized records of his spending on his expense account. He decides (not for the first time) that it's crazy that he pays for expenses his boss has told him the company will cover, and so he sets out to turn over a new leaf. Like a lot of people, he sometimes reads articles on becoming more organized and taking control of his finances, but the result of his reading is mostly that he sits and thinks. So he decides to take his effort to a higher level by practicing SODOTO.

First, seeing one. Who does he know who actually keeps records regularly? He begins talking to another member of his sales team about her habits. How often does she collect and record information? What does she do when she starts to fall behind? Seeing an "expert" at work provides Pete with insights and practical techniques that are different from what he has read about.

Second, doing one. Pete does a test run. For a month, he tries again to keep consistent records as he has learned to do from his research and from watching his colleague. Pete treats this month as a series of experiments. On Mondays he reviews his progress with his colleague, who is flattered that Pete wants her advice. After a week, Pete realizes that collecting his receipts and entering them into his personal finance software on his home computer at the end of the day is impractical—after a day at work, he can't bring himself to do it. He finds, though, that entering the data on his phone is almost fun, and it even clears his head after a meeting to do this small, mechanical task.

Finally, teaching one. A friend of Pete's meets him for a game of tennis and finds him sitting next to the court, entering data into his phone. Peter starts to explain his method to his friend and finds that when he has to explain the new habits he's trying to build, he sees the patterns in them more clearly and understands better why he's having more success. He also hears himself explaining that when he keeps up with this record keeping, he has a better sense of how he spends not just his expense account funds but his time. The record keeping has become a kind of work journal, helping him to notice when he is spending too much time on some sales accounts while neglecting others. SODOTO is helping him succeed.

chapter twenty-two

TAKE MULTIPLE SHOTS ON GOAL

Only a few weeks after I suggested that Kenji hedge his bets by seeking a job in a wider range of industries than energy, he emailed me about a job offer he had received. I was happy for him to have a bite so soon, but when I read the job description I was disappointed. The pay was on the low end and there was no connection to Asia. My gut sense was that this employer was bargain-hunting, assuming that with Kenji out of a job in the depths of a recession, he'd jump at anything. I told him: It looks to me like they're offering too little for a job you don't really want anyway. My advice is not to marry the first person who wants to kiss you. But of course, don't turn down the offer just because that's my advice. Seek out some real expertise first, including your own gut.

Kenji wrote back: "Everyone I trust says the same as you. But that's my only real offer—the rest are these little consulting opportunities, not really jobs at all. It's hard to turn down any offer when you've got nothing else." I understood what he meant, but I didn't think those other little consulting gigs were actually "nothing." Kenji said it was hard to tell what they might amount to—in fact, he wasn't even sure what to charge for them. At least one might not pay anything at all. But they had come through his network of businesspeople who were interested in Asia, and they all had some connection to an Asian company. I asked him to tell me more.

One part-time gig was with an energy start-up that had promising plans but was not yet up and running. Another was consulting to a division of his old company. The last was a temporary position at a Tier One electronics company. Increasingly, in electronics and other manufacturing areas, the company with its name on the outside of the product—say, a Sony television—doesn't actually make all the components on the inside. The company contracts out to specialized companies—Tier Ones—that make a flat screen or speakers or remote controls, and then assemble those pieces. The companies that make the pieces—the screen for the Sony TV, the headlights for the Jaguar, whatever it may be—are not identified. As a result, Tier One companies offer less prestige for their workers, yet they often produce high-quality work.

Kenji was reluctant to take the consulting position with the Tier One, because it was a very small job, offering neither the pay nor the prestige he was looking for. He thought these gigs were too small and the responsibilities were too vague—both big negatives for someone most at home with a Compete or blue approach. I asked if their small size might actually be their advantage. Then I suggested: Why don't you work on all of them? They may not amount to anything, but each shot on goal will increase your chances of success.

The analogy here is to hockey or soccer. Retired National Hockey League center Wayne Gretzky is still referred to as the Great One because he holds the record for the most goals scored and assisted, but what is often overlooked is that the top scorer also ranks near the top of the list for total shots on goal taken. In professional sports, most shots at the goal have a low chance of success because the defense is so good. To increase your odds, rather than trying to set up one perfect shot, make more attempts. The sheer number of attempts can put the odds on your side, and the winning team is often the one that managed more shots on goal, put more runners on base, or otherwise found more ways to try to score.

The late professor Ellis Paul Torrance came to a similar insight from his experimental research on highly creative people. He found that what set the most creative people apart was their greater fluency and flexibility in making attempts. Innovation, he found, is often a game of attrition. Just like the goldfish that lays five hundred eggs so that a few can thrive, we need to be willing not just to have a variety of targets but also to try repeatedly to hit each one.

Alison was a college student who seemed to understand the importance of shots on goal. She had an idea for a smartphone app she thought she could write and sell. She also had access to the equipment she needed in the college computer lab and friends willing to help her with the code and the testing. The obstacle she faced was finding uninterrupted time to work. Although she had a small amount of money saved, it wouldn't cover summer rent and her other living expenses. She considered renting a room in a shared apartment and then taking a part-time job, but she wanted the maximum number of hours to work on her app, total quiet while she worked, and enough living space that her long hours wouldn't make her crazy. She decided to look for less expensive housing for the summer.

Alison told everyone she knew that she was available for housesitting. She told her friends and her family; she told her professors. She listed her availability on social networking sites and some local websites. She hung paper signs on neighborhood billboards and telephone poles. In all these ways she was trying to take multiple shots on the same goal: housing in exchange for barter rather than money. But no one responded. Her friends and family were enthusiastic but had no useful connections. Strangers did not respond to her signs and postings. She began to feel discouraged.

One day, she mentioned her availability for the summer to some acquaintances she'd made at the local dog run, where she sometimes went because she missed her family dog. The dog owners were interested. Dog people like to leave their beloved pets with other dog people, and Alison was clearly one of them. As Alison had one enthusiastic chat after another about her summer scheme, she realized that she was getting a different kind of response. She stayed at the dog run that day for a couple of hours, stoking the conversation. One owner she knew only casually, impressed with Alison's obvious dedication to dogs and serious plan for the summer, told several professor friends at another school about Alison, and in time one met with Alison and asked her to take care of his dogs and his house while he traveled for the summer. Now Alison had not just rent-free accommodations but also a house where she could dedicate an entire room to her work. But she would never have hit her target had she not taken so many shots on goal. Of course, some apparent opportunities are only wastes of time, and some are flat out wrong: If you feel strongly that an opportunity is wrong, then turn it down. But making multiple attempts will give you the best chance to find what you're after.

If you struggle to come up with additional "shots" to take, it's often helpful to "think around the colors."

- YELLOW: COULD YOU COLLABORATE WITH OTHERS TO GET WHAT YOU'RE AFTER? Alison had tapped into her personal network of family, friends, and instructors.
- GREEN: COULD YOU TAKE A MORE CREATIVE APPROACH? Alison recognized that she had a special status among her local community of dog owners because they had seen how she came to the dog run to lavish attention on their pets and share stories about her own dog back home.
- BLUE: COULD YOU COMPETE FOR YOUR TARGET DIRECTLY? Alison competed for a house-sitting position in a variety of ways, such as posting paper notices and listing herself on websites.

- RED: COULD YOU USE A SYSTEM TO MAKE YOUR AP-
PROACH MORE EFFECTIVE? Allison joined the National
Association of Professional Pet Sitters and is listed in the
organization's pet sitter finder service to increase her
credibility and broaden her reach.

Thinking around the colors can be a powerful way to brainstorm
additional "shots" you can take on each target. The next few chapters suggest other ways to increase the number of shots you take.

chapter twenty-three

FAIL EARLY, FAIL OFTEN,
FAIL OFF-BROADWAY

Some years ago I was hired to help update a food product that all of us have known for years. A true household name, it nevertheless needed to change with the times. I'll call the product Trusty Bites. I worked with a team to develop Trusty Bites Millennium (TBM), an update on the classic product with a healthier recipe and a more modern look, while still keeping the old brand recognition, the old magic. When we had our first test version ready, we showed it to senior management. They loved it. They were so sure we had a winner that they wanted to debut TBM immediately, worldwide. This response was gratifying, but I said: Hold on. Let's take this more slowly. Let's pick a country in Eastern Europe or northern Africa and try the new formula and packaging there. It was a hard sell, but finally management agreed.

We launched TBM in Romania and it was a disaster. Fortunately, our failure was in a part of Eastern Europe, where our product wasn't well established, and the whole debacle went unnoticed by the major business media. So we went back to work, and when we had repaired the damage in Romania we took TBM, version two, to Italy. There it was a hit. Our success got reported and demand exploded—we had to rush the product to the rest of Europe and the United States. We couldn't ship it out fast enough. Now, of course, I looked like a genius. I'd helped save the brand! People in the company kept asking me: How did you know we would bomb in Romania?

I told them the truth. I hadn't known that. What I had known was that when you innovate, you need to run experiments, and what most experiments do is fail. Failure is an inevitable part of innovation, so you have to build in a place and a time for it. In the last chapter I said that Wayne Gretzky became the top scorer in hockey by taking more shots on goal than any other player, but if you take more shots on goal, you're also going to have more misses. And in fact, Gretzky was not just the top scorer in the NHL; he was also one of the leaders in missed shots. Pelé missed the goal more than almost any player in soccer. Babe Ruth is remembered as the home run king, but he was also a strikeout king. They all succeeded by failing more than other players.

Artists understand this as well. When Alan Jay Lerner and Frederick Loewe opened their new musical *Camelot* in Toronto in 1960, the curtain came down four and half hours after the opening number—the show was more than twice as long as any commercially viable Broadway show. The play then moved to Boston, still far from the New York theater critics, where acts and songs were cut, but the run time was still an hour too long. Finally, when it reached the Majestic Theatre on Broadway, *Camelot* was down to about half of its original length. It went on to become a blockbuster success, a classic of musical theater that is still produced today.

Like most great artisans, Lerner and Loewe understood that failure is an inevitable part of the act of creation. The real failure is to try to avoid failure because only by failing do you discover where the problems are. The great successes come not by avoiding failure but by accelerating it. That's why I say fail more and faster, but do it out of sight. Just like learning a new language or playing an instrument you've never touched before, you're going to make a mess of it when you start. So make a big mess, make it fast, and keep it hidden. Effortless superiority is only for those who trod the safely beaten path. We innovators must fail our way to success.

This was the logic behind the approach that Teri, the baker, took when she began offering her creations at a local restaurant, a farmer's market, and at her old school's cafeteria and fund-raising events. These settings gave her the chance to test out her wares and see what actual customers tasted and enjoyed and bought. It was still early in her attempt to make baking her career, and she had many failures, but she was far away from "Broadway"—no one who took a sample of her rock-hard oatmeal–peanut butter squares at the school carnival was going to hold that against her in a year or two when she opened her own store.

Most people seem relieved when I tell them it's all right, in fact necessary, to fail more, but it can be hard to apply this rule to personal situations. Some otherwise gifted innovators hesitate to risk failure in their personal lives because they can never get far enough from "Broadway."

Children, too, need to be able to fail "Off-Broadway." Whether that means trying a new sport and being the worst player on the team for a while or taking an advanced course and struggling to catch up to the rest of the class, children must have space to fall down and pick themselves up again without crushing criticism or shame. It's not just that failure is tolerable—it's the fastest road to improvement. But if kids are made to feel that they must not fail in front of their parents or teachers, they may become so risk-averse that they avoid activities unless they're sure they can succeed. They wind up repeating their past successes, limiting their chances to learn, and losing track of their own purpose. Instead, they make a near religion out of playing it safe. When playing it safe is impossible, their overreliance on this Control approach may push them into the negative zone, in the worst cases to the point of suicide. We need to make sure that the people we keep close to us understand the importance not just of running experiments but also of tolerating—even welcoming—their necessary failures.

chapter twenty-four

SHOW, DON'T TELL

Kenji's job search was still moving slowly, so he decided to take my suggestion that he accept all three consulting gigs while he was out of work. He didn't make a lot of money from them, and two of the jobs never amounted to much—as I've said, most experiments fail. But the marketing work he did for the Tier One company got noticed by one customer, a very well-known Korean electronics company. After a successful season, that Korean electronics company offered him a full-time job. It was unusual for a Korean company to hire a Japanese-American, and perhaps if Kenji had gone through the usual job-search process, he might not have gotten an offer. Working for the Tier One had never been Kenji's goal, but the part-time gig became his chance to show other companies what he could do. He had found a way to show, not tell: The company already knew him and his work, and he was able to negotiate a full-time marketing position that met his target fully. He sent me a note a few months later saying, "This is the best job I've ever had!"

From the musician who hands a record company executive a demo recording in an elevator to the intern in any organization who shows what he or she can do before applying for a paying job, "show, don't tell" is a powerful means for increasing the number of shots you take on goal. There are three basic elements to this approach:

1. *Create a story about what you have done and put the person you want to influence in the story.* Recently, for example, a young Twitter follower of mine, someone I'd never met, emailed to say that he was interested in my work but unimpressed with my website. Someone like you, he said, ought to have something very different in your video presentations. He was telling me a story about me, and it was a story I wanted to hear more about. I answered his email.

2. *Offer some material evidence.* Drawings, pen-and-paper sketches, models, audio and video recordings, and websites are all relatively inexpensive, yet they have huge psychological impact. Most of the brain is used to make sense of pictures, so offer something people can see. My Twitter follower sent me some sample video and webpage mock-ups that he had created.

3. *Relate what you can offer to what the other person needs.* My Twitter follower sent me a note along with examples of his work, saying, "Your video should look more like this. Your website should be more like this." I watched his samples and I thought yes, that's very good. So I hired him to do Web-related work for this book. Had he contacted me the usual way, with a résumé and a letter, I probably never would have gotten the chance to see how well his skills suited my needs. But he didn't tell me he wanted to work for me. He showed me what he could do for me. And so I made room for him in my life.

Although the most common examples of "show, don't tell" tend to be stories of new ventures—seeking a job or winning an audience for an unknown creative work—that doesn't mean this innovation method is only helpful to the young or unproven. Recently I was approached by a successful friend in the area of finance who was interested in partnering with the White House on an initiative. He said: You've done some work with some people connected to this administration. Do you know anyone who could make some introductions?

I said I wouldn't recommend taking that approach. Even though I knew people who might be able to make an introduction, I also knew that you can't get the attention of the White House that way. Everyone wants to be introduced to the president. You need to show the White House what you can do for them. Pick a state that's going through the kind of financial difficulties you want to work on nationally and offer that state your help. Get some results at the state level. Then you'll be riding something that's already in motion, and people who are concerned about similar issues at the national level—even the president himself—may want to learn how you helped move an individual state forward. Instead of asking for an introduction, try "show, don't tell"—and they'll ask to meet you.

chapter twenty-five

YOU ARE THE STAR
ONLY IN YOUR OWN MOVIE

You may be wondering by now how you are supposed to use all of this advice. Not just one target but several. Not just one shot at each target but multiple shots. Advice from experts. Samples to show, not just tell, what you can do. Who has time for it all? Running experiments makes most of us wish we had a team playing with us, an ensemble to support us in the drama of remaking our lives. That's why top companies organize teams to innovate together. At General Electric, I helped the company work on what they called "imagination breakthroughs." The company funded these efforts heavily, investing tens of millions of dollars to motivate different divisions of the company to work together to meet goals on a common project. Everyone involved was evaluated on meeting the shared goals and rewarded for doing so in their year-end bonuses. The results were enormous, but what good is that for the individual innovator who has no team and no millions?

To start, it's a reminder that most innovations require support from others. And it's a clue about how to inspire that kind of support: Provide incentives. The fact is almost nobody cares about you. People aren't terribly concerned about the role you're going to play or whether you succeed in it. But they are concerned about how your role fits with their role. They will work with you if you help them succeed in their own "movies."

The fact is, even if you do run a team, they still think of themselves as the stars in the movie. The famous principle of sacrifice for the group—"Take one for the team"—is actually rubbish. Most people don't sacrifice themselves for the team. They work for the team because they believe that the team is also working for them. I am a good member of my university community because I know that I must contribute to the well-being of the community just as the community needs to support my own work. Every day there are things that are annoying or that don't go exactly my way, but I negotiate and compromise and act like an adult as much as reasonably possible. It's true in marriages—we don't always get exactly what we want moment by moment, but we negotiate our way through because we love each other, have shared commitments, and have the deep feeling that we are better off together than apart.

Take time away from thinking about your targets to think about what motivates the people you need working with you. Each of us feels, at least some of the time, that the great movie of existence began when we were born and that the great drama is whether we will succeed. But you are the star only in your own movie: To almost everyone else, you're just another member of the ensemble. You have to create roles for the others whom you want to play a part in your story. Give them reasons to choose to meet your goals, even if you don't have a multimillion-dollar budget for team building. When you want someone else to partner with you in any kind of innovation, try to imagine the movie as if the other person were the star. What quest is that person on? What sort of allies does he or she need? Can you present what you need in such a way that it serves those needs? This is the way to build an ensemble cast of top actors so you can have the best allies possible as you run your experiments.

Ronnie wanted to open a restaurant, and he saw that others who succeeded in this high-risk business often had a mentor—an older, more successful restaurateur who provided advice and practical suggestions. But when it came to finding a mentor, Ronnie couldn't get past the nagging question of why anyone would want to give up their valuable time to help him. I told him: In a way, you're right. If you approach potential mentors by saying, "Excuse me, sorry to bother you, but I'm scared I'm going to fail. Would you mind giving up some of your precious time for a nobody like me?" then you're right, they'll say no. So you need to stop thinking about this as the movie *Will Ronnie Succeed?* Think of it instead as their movie: They've learned the hard way. They've persevered and succeeded. And at this point in their career, they feel a desire to tell their stories and share what they have learned, in part so they can relive the excitement of the early years again, this time not as a player but as a coach. Don't go begging for their time. Offer them the chance to play a great new role, that of the admired and respected coach.

One practical lesson here is that what tends to attract others to be part of your "movie" is your strengths. Others will want to share in what you do well or in the resources you can offer. In this I agree with Marcus Buckingham and Donald Clifton, in their book *Now, Discover Your Strengths*, that it is a mistake to assume success will come when you improve your areas of weakness. If I am a mediocre actor but a great movie director and I'm looking for great actors to be in my movie, I will do far better offering to direct their movie than in trying to overcome my weaknesses, become a great actor myself, and join their acting company as a player. Similarly, if I'm a great hitter but weak in the field, I'll assemble the strongest team by finding good fielders who want to be on a team with a great hitter. Nobody has total range, so what's necessary is to use your strengths to attract those with complementary strengths. Think of the superhero team, the Fantastic Four: Having one super skill doesn't mean you have to develop the others'. If your unique ability is flying with flames, let someone else create invisible force fields.

Consider the experiment you're trying to run next. Are you hesitating because you lack some understanding or talent? Have you put off some deadline until you master some skill or acquire some new area of expertise? Sometimes the need to answer one practical question can delay a personal project for months. Rather than focusing on self-improvement, focus on the experiment. You may be the star of your movie, but that doesn't mean you have to play Superman. Find someone else who can benefit from a strength you already have and let that person be the star in this "scene." Let that person make the complex judgment or take the tricky shot. In Ronnie's case, once he had a mentor, he let the mentor guide him through all his negotiations, from his real estate contract to his arrangements with his day and night managers. Ronnie was a promising chef, but he was inexperienced in negotiation, so he let his mentor take the starring role in those "scenes." That's how capable people move their stories forward.

chapter twenty-six

THE MONGOLIAN BARBECUE EFFECT

I was one of the key architects of the merger between two old, proud hospitals. Neither hospital was in a financial position to survive on its own, so the practical question was how to combine the two organizations to preserve their strengths while cutting out weak areas and redundancies. Yet even though that was the practical question, as I worked with them it became clear that the real challenge was *not* how to draw up a merger plan—that was going to be relatively easy. The challenge was to get these proud and highly territorial rivals to agree to do anything with each other.

The situation made me think of the Mongolian barbecue joint near where I live. When you eat there, you can cook your own food on your own griddle. It's enormously popular—more popular, in fact, than the four-star Chinese restaurant nearby, which my "foodie" Chinese wife tells me is a truly remarkable Chinese restaurant. But more people go to Mongolian barbecue because they would rather eat what they cook themselves. They trust it because they make it with their own hands and they feel a pride of ownership, even if they know nothing about cooking. It's their own.

To broker the hospital merger, I brought together teams from both hospitals. I guided them through a process of agreeing to shared goals and principles, and then I let them make the hard choices for the merger plan themselves. Now we all had the benefit of the Mongolian barbecue effect: They were satisfied with what we'd made because they'd helped to make it.

If you are trying to get people to work with you as you run your experiments and you encounter resistance, you may feel an impulse to take charge and tell them exactly how to do what you want them to do. But when you need a group to agree, there is nothing as powerful as involving the people who will be affected by the decisions they make and will have to live with. It's as true of doctors, nurses, and administrators as it is of little children. Let them share in the planning and the cooking. Let them get their hands dirty and make some of their own decisions. They will be a lot more likely to accept the results.

chapter twenty-seven

——

HIDE INSIDE TROJAN HORSES

Sometimes, even if you try all of the approaches I have just mentioned, it will seem that you can't get anyone to help run your next experiment. No one wants to see what you've got to show. No one wants you in their movie, not even in a bit part. No one will meet you at the Mongolian barbecue. I felt this frustration when I was doing consulting work for a pharmaceutical company that was developing new drugs. I felt certain that my team had innovative approaches that could do great things for the company, but even though I'd been hired as a consultant to help them find new ways to innovate and come up with new ways to approach their process, no one was listening. Of course, every citadel has its gates to keep out the foreigners, with guards who patrol the walls day and night. In business, those guards uses catchphrases like "We need more data" or "We don't have the time or money right now" or that showstopper, "We need to send this to committee to get authorization." The translation of all of these is the same: No, never. Yet these custodians of the old way and barriers to the new can be outdone.

At the pharmaceutical company, I heard every version of "no." How could I get past the gates and into the city? I decided to get back to creativizing basics. Were there projects at the company that were on a roll or going very badly? I heard about some that were going well—they showed promising early results, well ahead of schedule—but though their teams were on a roll, they didn't see any reason to let me benefit from it. I also learned about one drug in development that was offtrack—not that it was ineffective or unsafe, but its development was way too slow. The senior scientist had gotten hired away by another firm and the team kept missing its deadlines for FDA approvals, without which they could never bring the drug to market and make any money.

I went to the head of that team, who was feeling the pain of failing in front of her peers. Drug discovery is expensive—costs for one drug can run from half a billion dollars to twice that, sometimes more. No one wants to be responsible for wasting that kind of money. I offered to share some of the alternative methods that my innovation team had devised. It should already be clear what was in it for the team leader. She was in a bad situation, so, for her, risk and reward had reversed: She had lots to gain and nothing to lose. But if she needed to creativize, what did I need? I needed a Trojan horse, something I could do for the company that I could hide inside while I sneaked past the guards at the gates, so I could get inside the city where my real target lay. I had no connection to this particular drug in development and I had no relationship with this failing team, but helping them was a way I could get where I was trying to go.

Many opportunities are like Trojan horses: They may not have anything to do with your real goals, but if you hide inside them, they will get you inside the gates. Once you're inside, you will find new opportunities you could never have reached from the outside. Because this team was motivated to avoid failure and was hungry for some fresh leadership after the departure of the head scientist on the team, they embraced my new methods. We got to work and in the end the drug came in on schedule. It never rocked the industry or made a lot of money, but the team was happy to turn their bad performance around, and now I was on the inside, part of the company story: People in the company heard about what we had done and

wanted to know how we'd done it. Our new practices for drug discovery were adopted in pieces by other divisions of the company. We
were able to prove that our new methods could bring a higher level
of success to a major pharmaceutical company—and that had been
my target all along.

The Trojan horse has a bad reputation—in the original Greek
story, the enormous wooden horse was a gift that tricked King Priam
into letting the enemy soldiers inside the horse come inside the de-
fensive walls of his city. In the age of the personal computer, a Trojan is a piece of malicious software that appears benign, but steals
information or damages the system on which it is installed. Those
are both harmful uses of the underlying innovation technique, but
the technique itself deserves our respect because it works with people and organizations who would otherwise never give us a chance.
When you devise a Trojan horse, many of the worst features in your
innovation landscape suddenly look like opportunities. Do you have
an incompetent boss, colleague, or friend whose mistakes keeps you
from making the connections you want to make? Help that person to
succeed and you will get access to their world—their resources, their
contacts, their thinking, and possibly even their future projects. Inside a Trojan horse project, you can ride with them.

Ben Franklin was a master of the Trojan horse. Although not a
religiously observant man himself, the Founding Father contributed
to every church built in Philadelphia in his lifetime. Once he made
himself welcome in a church, he could find the personal allies and the
investors he needed for his many projects, which also benefited the
Philadelphia community. Like joining a knitting circle to make new
friends, volunteering to clean up the local park as a way to network
with your neighbors, or working for the block association as a step
toward a local political run, Franklin's donations were Trojan horse
schemes, but schemes that did good for everyone involved.

chapter twenty-eight

LEARN FROM EXPERIENCE
AND EXPERIMENTS

If you're driving through a midwestern snowstorm and your car gets stuck, you'll likely discover two things. The first, which often makes travelers happy, is that many midwesterners will stop for you. They'll climb out of their cars and walk into the blowing storm to help you get your car out of the ditch. The second, which often makes travelers unhappy, is that before they give you a push or a tow, midwesterners are likely to offer up a frank review of your situation. You're going to find out what you did wrong. "You really thought four-wheel drive was going to work in weather like this? Didn't you ever hear of snow tires?"

As a midwesterner myself, I've heard more than one visitor ask how it is that the same person can be so helpful and so rude. But to me those remarks aren't rude. To me they sound like what they call in the military an "after-action review." You tried something, you saw action of some kind, so now let's review it, honestly and objectively. I think of this as prismatic thinking in reverse. Instead of "thinking around the colors" to find what you could do differently, now you consider what you tried in each of the four categories—Collaborate, Create, Compete, and Control—and for each one you ask four questions:

• WHAT WORKED? Whatever it is that worked is what you should do more of, next time. Very often the successful "color" of the approach or the specific shot on goal won't be the one you expected: Alison, who was designing an app, had assumed at first that she'd find a house-sitting position through her online postings. When she began to get positive responses from fellow dog lovers, it came as a surprise. But she understood that the approach that succeeds is the one that deserves more of your time, resources, and effort. It's not even necessary that you can explain *why* it works, only that you let your experiments guide your future actions. Alison decided to stop hanging paper signs and instead to spend an entire afternoon at the dog run, playing with dogs, meeting their owners, and telling them about her situation.

Doing more of what works may sound simple enough, but the challenge here—and one of the biggest mistakes poor innovators make—is that what works isn't necessarily what we expect to work. When you review your results, the point is not to ask, "Did the experiment succeed in the way I planned?" The point is to ask instead, "Is anything here helpful or worth repeating?" From champagne to penicillin, from Teflon to Post-it notes to Viagra, many of the most famous and profitable innovations in the history of business were accidents discovered in the pursuit of other goals. So leave room for the surprise discovery. Great painters talk about the point at which they stop painting the picture and the picture seems to paint itself. Innovation resembles the making of art because at its core, it's what we call ambiguous and emergent: You don't know what will succeed and you don't know when it will appear. Innovation is not just about making something new or improved; it's about making it up as you go along. The wise innovator leaves the door of expectations open and welcomes unplanned visitors.

• WHAT DIDN'T WORK? Whatever didn't work, even if you expected it to succeed, is what you should do less of. Because when it comes to specific methods, if it doesn't work the first time, chances are it never will. Remember the venture capital model I described: You can't keep giving more and more money to twelve different companies—you'll go broke before you ever see results. For that reason, when you try an approach and it doesn't work, accept the loss, let the experiment go, and put your resources elsewhere. This is true even if you thought at the beginning that you had a winner. Trust your results, not your expectations or your original plan. When it comes to innovation, only the idiot sticks to the plan.

Of course, for those few failed attempts that seem to deserve a second try, you need to ask: What improvements would make it worth another shot? And that brings us to our next question.

• WHAT SIMPLE LESSONS CAN WE LEARN? This is the key. The point of the after-action review is not scorekeeping. Don't just tally up successes and failures from your experiments; get smarter by turning those results into simple rules of thumb for the future. Alison realized that dog lovers want their pets cared for with love when they're away. Her obvious enthusiasm and comfort around dogs was the perfect job recommendation. So instead of hanging more signs for people who had no idea who she was or why they would want her in their lives, she focused on a group of people who valued her as a dog person.

Similarly, at the Innovatrium, my innovation lab, we found that there was something that mattered to our customers besides the quality of the guidance and the innovative ideas we helped provide: frequent contact. Clients who heard from us on a regular basis tended to stick around. Clients who went too long without hearing from us were more likely to wander, even when our work for them was excellent. And so in a review session we came up with these two rules: First, if a client asks for a proposal explaining how we would do new work, we should deliver that proposal in no more than forty-eight hours. Second, no matter what stage of the work we might be in, a client should never go more than a week without hearing from someone in our shop. With these two rules, we boiled down our accidental experiments in customer contact—sometimes we were in touch, sometimes we weren't—into two simple lessons.

• WHAT CAN YOU TRY DIFFERENTLY NEXT TIME? Once you have distilled simple lessons based on your experiments, then you're ready to start the cycle over again, using those lessons to help you set new targets, seeking relevant experts and partners, and running new experiments. At the Innovatrium, we had to ask ourselves: Now that we have learned these simple lessons, who should be in charge of maintaining contact with clients in the future? Who in the company (or at the client) understood their need for communication best? What specific changes did we need to make in order to put these rules into practice? Our next experiments were in part attempts to answer those questions. And the cycles continued, making us a tighter, smarter, and more innovative group with each small change we made.

innovation is not an IQ test

When you list the four questions, as I've just done, it sounds simple enough—maybe it even sounds obvious. Who *wouldn't* take the time to do a little thinking, get smarter, and innovate better? Wouldn't you rather have a short, somewhat uncomfortable conversation with the guy who pulled your car out of a ditch than wind up stuck again during the next raging midwestern storm? And yet, many innovators who understand the concept of the after-action review fail to show up for it. Repeatedly in my work I have seen smart, creative people falter and fail at innovation, while relatively less intelligent, less creative people succeed. And the reason those less talented people sometimes outperform the ones with more ideas and more skills is that innovation is not an IQ test or a talent show; innovation is a cyclical learning process. It's more effective to have three or four ideas, test them out, observe which one gets measurable results, and then give that approach all you've got than it is to have a thousand ideas or brilliant analytical insights that never change what you do day to day.

Completing an after-action review is often trickier than we might imagine. Harvard Business School professor Gerald Zaltman and researcher Lindsay Zaltman studied leadership and made a remarkable discovery: Corporate leaders typically fail to think deeply. They just march their organizations in the directions they were already going. They don't conduct after-action reviews and they don't distill rules to follow the next time, and so they never improve their approach. Why not? Zaltman and Zaltman found four reasons.

First, there is a trade-off between the short term and the long term. In the long term, learning and changing make it easier to succeed. But in the short term, it's going to be more work. And leaders, like other human beings, tend to avoid work if they can get away with it.

Second, to think differently, you're going to have to undergo some personal discomfort and that, too, is something most of us automatically tend to avoid. A business consultant I know likes to say that before his organization can plan a new strategy with a client's CEO, there is something that has to happen first: The CEO has to cry. He or she has to realize that what he thought was a great idea wasn't, and that the people working for the company have been suffering. If you've ever watched the television program *Undercover Boss*, you'll know what I mean: When the CEO watches the secret recordings of what's really going on in his or her own company, it's painful. And most leaders, like other human beings, tend to avoid pain.

Third, real thought involves changing your mind, and all decisions have costs. You may decide it's more meaningful to leave your corporate position in order to teach in the inner city, but you will have to do so at a fraction of the pay. You may decide that the brilliant prototype you built in your garage can't really be turned into a full-scale business, but then you have to let go of five years of work. You may decide you would be happiest living in a small town, but then you have to say goodbye to your friends and neighbors in the city. Every change in understanding has a cost.

Finally, reviewing is useless without real information. Many people spin theories but they don't test out their theories against data. In our terms, this means that not only do many innovators fail to show up for the after-action review, but many who do show up don't bring their observations of what went right and wrong with their experiments. So although they feel that they are doing important thinking, in fact they are just preaching to the choir. Listen to talk radio on either end of the political spectrum. It's mostly answers, a few questions, and almost no actual data. No one ever gets the chance to change his mind.

Those are the reasons that leaders of companies fail to think effectively. Of course, when it comes to innovating your own life, the leader who matters is you. If you get caught in my hypothetical snowstorm, you'll have no choice but to listen to the review—the price of getting pulled out of the ditch is listening to what your rescuer says about you. But in ordinary life, it's easy to hide from the after-action review—or to sabotage it if someone else tries to force one. So it's up to you to buck the trend and be one of those rare, excellent leaders willing to engage in deep thinking.

RULES FOR AN AFTER-ACTION REVIEW

• TALK IT THROUGH WITH A NEUTRAL COMPANION. Once you have run some experiments and you're ready to ask and answer the questions I listed above—what worked, what didn't, what simple lessons you can learn, and what you could do differently in the next round of experiments—don't conduct your review alone. If you are having trouble looking at your results, find someone to keep you company and encourage you. If you're having trouble being objective, get someone who cares about you to help you look at it objectively. The person with whom you ask those four questions should be someone who doesn't have a stake in the outcome, someone you trust who knows you and wants you to succeed but who isn't relying on you to succeed in this particular round of experiments. You may need to rule out your business partner, your soul mate, or your best friend who just invested in your new business. The key is to find someone neutral: a friend, mentor, or formal coach with no stake in what you choose. Clio, whose job and love affair in Boston had both run their course, didn't have that sort of friend or mentor, so she hired a personal coach. He encouraged her to see her vacation to the Southwest not as an escape but as a first attempt at researching and planning a new life.

• MAKE SURE YOU DO MOST OF THE TALKING. Even at the Innovatrium, where we have been hired to make a company's innovations more successful, we sit down with our clients and we ask them to go around the room and come up with their own reflections on what worked, what didn't, what rules they can divine, and what changes they want to make for the future. This is the crux of how innovation really works because this is the chance for the participants to get smarter about their own efforts: By doing your own learning, you increase your capability to innovate well in the future. That's why you need to do the thinking, the talking, and the acting for yourself. Clio's life coach was careful to spend a lot of time listening to her express her frustrations and her hopes. Then, when she raised the possibility of leaving her company in Boston to become a consultant based in the Southwest, he helped her hear that she was voicing not just a daydream but a possibility: "You know," he said, "you could take the initiative." Then he started to help her make a plan.

• NO CARROTS, NO STICKS. If you offer rewards for "good" results or punishments for "bad" ones, you will immediately distort the review. Most people offered carrots or sticks, even without meaning to, will find that they become greedy or fearful or both. To compensate for those powerful feelings, they will stretch the truth, exaggerate what doesn't matter, place blame, and otherwise muddy the waters where you are trying to see which experiments worked and what to do differently next time. The best results come when you and the person you are talking to can maintain a Buddhist-like calm: impersonal, highly focused, but with a background feeling of kindness. As a rule, if you find the experience of your after-action review either painful or exhilarating, then you know it has lost focus. Try it again with someone who can help you be focused but impersonal.

• LIST WHAT YOU LEARN. As you come up with simple rules of thumb based on the experiments you've already run, write them down. Make your own recipe. On Clio's "scouting mission" to Arizona and New Mexico, she visited a cousin in Tucson and quickly discovered that living at sea level in the desert was too hot for her; if she was going to live in the Southwest, it would have to be in the mountains. That was another line for her "recipe." She made a new list of cities to visit, and rented a car to explore them.

Personally, I like to fill a page with what I've learned, along with an inspirational quote, possibly something memorable my mom once said, maybe an old saw that seems newly relevant to my situation, such as "measure twice, cut once." I type these few sentences up and then take them to the local copy center to be laminated so I can hang them on my office wall. I need to see them to remember to use them. By now, the people at the copy center know me very well.

• CHOOSE SOMEONE TO HELP YOU FOLLOW YOUR OWN LIST. Some of us need reminding. Some of us need to be encouraged to look a little harder at ourselves. Some need to stop being so hard on ourselves. But for almost all of us, it's useful to have a partner or buddy to help us integrate what we have learned from an after-action review yesterday into our ongoing efforts today and tomorrow. This might be the same person who helped you conduct the review, but it might be a separate person, a "designated implementer." In general, the person you are looking for here is not a drill sergeant. The most useful attitude, again, seems to be one of emotional detachment with a little bias toward kindness, someone who can help you feel about yourself: *I'm a good person, there's nothing wrong with my life, but I'm not as effective as I could be at innovating solo, so I'm going to enlist someone to help me.*

• REVIEW ACTIONS, NOT INTENTIONS. Sometimes it's tempting to tell people about your experiments before you've even run them. But while it's useful to seek appropriate expertise before trying something new, as I described a few chapters ago, it's actually dangerous to share your intentions and hopes before you've made your practical attempts. The risk here is known in psychological research as "secondary gain." If someone has a goal—let's say training for a marathon—and that person tells others about it and gets lots of positive feedback for his or her plans, that person actually becomes *less likely* to reach the goal. The secondary benefits they get from talking about it makes them feel so good, they no longer feel as much urgency to act. So don't let your after-action review become a chance to be admired for your future plans. Keep the focus on the experiments you've already run.

chapter twenty-nine

WHEN NOTHING SEEMS TO WORK

Javier was lamenting his impossibly busy workdays. A vice president at a large corporation, he found that his work was constantly interrupted by the people who reported to him. Running his department was like having thirty children, he said, every one with a question he needed to help answer or a fire he needed to help put out. I'd talked to him in the past about innovating his way out of this counterproductive situation. We'd explored some experiments he could run: limiting the times of day when he was available or establishing alternative problem-solving resources for his people, such as formal peer-to-peer guidance. He'd set some targets and run some experiments, but now he told me that "none of that stuff" really made a difference. He'd tried limiting access to himself, and he'd offered them all kinds of alternate strategies for solving the problems that came up, but it just seemed that none of them could handle anything for themselves. And so, he told me, he had to keep handling it for them.

Of course, he knew his work situation better than I did. I wasn't going to tell him how to do his job. And I could hear, clearly, that he had a very logical explanation for why all his experiments had failed and no innovation was going to change things. But rather than making me agree with him that the case was, in effect, closed, his very logical explanation made me suspicious.

What does it mean when none of your experiments works? Up to now, I've made it sound as if one will always succeed. But what do you do when you have three or four horses in a race and all of them lose? That might mean you are stuck with an impossible problem. Maybe there is no innovation in the world that can help you. But it might also be that your thinking is dominated by a false logic. In that case, before you can innovate a solution, you have to innovate your thinking and escape that logic.

Imagine you go to a doctor who makes a wrong diagnosis of your illness. You really are ill, but he's wrong about what's making you sick. Based on his wrong diagnosis, he prescribes the recommended treatment for a disease you don't have. Over time, he may have you try all the possible treatments for that disease, but it's still not the disease that you have. In the end, he may conclude that you have a rare form of the disease that resists treatment. The point I want to make about this doctor is that he's done everything right except the diagnosis, and as a result everything else he's done is wrong, even though he's following his medical training perfectly. I've seen this same kind of error sometimes among consultants I work with. They'll say things like: *This client is too dumb to realize his problem!* When I hear that, an alarm goes off in my head. I wonder: Is it the client who's not sharp enough to realize what a genius you are, or is it the consultant who is too stuck in dominant logic to realize he or she has missed the real problem?

The smarter people are, I've found, the more likely they are to be fooled by their favorite dominant logic. That's because the dominant logic has been so successful for them in the past that they've come to trust it. It's not necessarily wrong, stupid, or manipulative, though it may be all of those things. It's essentially a story about some part of the world that makes sense from a certain perspective—but that perspective is not yours.

If you're paying attention when you take a commercial airline flight, for example, you'll notice that while your ticket might say that the flight lasts two hours, once you're on board the captain will announce that your flight time is barely more than one hour. So why did the airline tell you it was a two-hour flight and make you come to the airport earlier? The answer is that those departure and arrival times are written by and for the airlines. Airlines compete with each other for on-time performance, and they look bad when their flights are late. So at some point a person at one of the airlines realized that if they exaggerated the lengths of the flights, they would be able to report more on-time arrivals. And that's what they do. Many people never notice that their "on-time" flight actually took longer than the "late" flight they might have taken several years ago. Similarly, why is checkout time at a hotel in mid-morning? It's often inconvenient for the traveler. But it's helpful for the hotel, because they want to have time to bring housekeeping in to clean up. The logic suits their perspectives and their needs, even if it doesn't always suit yours.

Dominant logic is complicated because we're not actually rational beings, even though some economists still like to pretend that we are. As a result, it's necessary to be skeptical about the reasons people give for what they do. An associate was saying to me recently that the reason he's going to buy a time-share in Florida is that it's cheaper than a hotel. That's perfectly logical, but it's not his real reason. I know him pretty well, and I know that he may not even use his week when it comes around. I'd bet quite a bit that the real reason he bought the time-share is to fuel a fantasy. He lives in Michigan but he has a lot of wealthy friends who have several houses, and often at least one of those houses is in a warm climate. By buying a one-week time-share, this friend of mine gets to feel as if he has a condo in Florida like his rich friends. He gets to feed his fantasy of being a wealthier person than he is.

Or think about cars. The purpose of a car is to provide reliable and safe transportation. That is what an economist would call the "absolute value proposition" of a car. If humans were rational beings, we would pay the most for cars that are the most reliable and the safest. But in fact, the most expensive cars break down a lot, aren't very safe, require premium gas, and so forth. So why do we buy expensive cars? I'm not trying to play Freud here, but my point is that there are other kinds of logic at work. What this means, as a practical matter, is that you need to be skeptical of the stories people tell you about the situations they're in—including the stories they tell about innovations that aren't working.

Very often, I'll go to a meeting with a potential client and I'll be told a great-sounding story about how the entire company is united in its desire to innovate and how much they want to work with me personally. The CEO is fully behind this, and the finance people all agree that it's essential to focus on innovation, and blah, blah, blah. Sometimes that's true. But sometimes I arrive and I look around the room, and it turns out the CEO got called away at the last minute, and the chief financial officer couldn't make it either, and I realize that the true story is not the one I've been told. The people who show up for the meeting are the ones who are committed to the project (or who don't have the stature in the company to skip it)—the other ones were just paying lip service to a fine-sounding story that hides the dominant logic of the company.

When it comes to personal innovation, though, you don't usually have a room to look around and see who's really on board and who isn't. You have a story you've been telling yourself in your head and you have conflicting feelings and obligations, also in your head. Like my manager friend Javier who felt he couldn't escape the childlike neediness of his thirty employees, the solo innovator has mainly him- or herself to rely on to get the story straight. So how do you know, when none of your experiments has worked, if your goal is unreachable or if you're stuck in dominant logic?

Start with a test. Think of a situation in which you want to innovate but it's been rough going. You've been working on this for a long time. Maybe you've set targets and made attempts and missed and vowed to try again.

Describe the situation in a sentence or two.

Now describe what's holding you back. What goes wrong? Try to give an explanation as quickly as you give the problem. Do it in twenty seconds or less.

Were you able to do it? If so, then chances are you're stuck in a dominant logic that's blinding you to other critical issues. If the challenge you face was as quick and simple as your explanation, chances are you would have solved it by now. And if you can analyze it that quickly, you're probably not analyzing it at all.

Seeing a familiar problem fresh and making new sense out of situations we thought we already understood is slow work. But it is a kind of innovation—you are innovating a new perspective on your own story—and so it responds to the innovation technique we've been using throughout this book. It happens in stages and often over time. But how?

break through dominant logic
with the Russian nesting dolls

Often people stuck in dominant logic are also stuck at the personal level. They say: I've tried everything. Or they say: I know I can do better. I'll just have to try harder. I, I, I, I. That's a clue that you need to consider the other levels, the larger nesting dolls. Again, it helps to think of the story you are telling yourself.

At the universal level, every story has a setting. Where are we? What is the weather like? What's moving and what's dying? At the start of a Western, we are usually given a shot that establishes the universal level, the setting of the story; the desert landscape with the small frontier town in background. Right away we know that certain things are possible and others are not—this is not a story that will end with a socialist revolution, for example. In the case of Javier, his industry was going through a profound adjustment in a difficult economy. That change at the universal level meant that everyone in the company felt anxiety not just for their job but for the future relevance of their skills.

At the community level, every story has certain character types who may appear and those who may not. A Western may have a sheriff, a deputy, a saloon owner, and so forth. It is not going to have a lot of sailors or astronauts. Javier had taken on the role of adviser, almost of a father figure, to the anxious workers who reported to him at a time of severe change. But was that the only character he could play? Was it even a useful character for him to play? He might well have been right in feeling that his employees were insecure about their jobs and their competence, and he might have been responding to those needs, but maybe he was the wrong one to respond. Someone else—an expert on the future of the industry, say, or even someone with psychological training who could address the anxiety and low morale—might be available who could better play this role than Javier. The fact that playing this role for so long was frustrating to him was all the sign we needed to see that he needed to make a change.

Finally, as we move from the community back to the individual level, in every story there are various actions that can be taken, and in various sequences. Innovation is like cooking: It's not just a matter of putting all the right ingredients in a pot. You also have to cover the pot or stir its contents, turn the heat up or down, and you have to do these things in a certain order. From my point of view, Javier had the right ingredients but the wrong chef in the kitchen, getting the order of the steps wrong.

I told him: Let's assume you're right and your people have these needs. Find someone else who can address their needs. If they need retraining, get them retraining. If they need counseling, encourage them to get counseling. But you are their boss, and you hired them to do their jobs; and when they come to you feeling that they can't handle their work, it's up to you to say: You know what? I'm your boss and I hired you because you can handle it. Don't come to me to approve every small decision. That way all of us can get more done and we might just ride out this difficult period.

Sheila came to me when her plan to become a doctor seemed like it would fail. She had been a good student in college, and now she was enrolled in a special course for college graduates without science backgrounds—"pre-med for poets"—but even so she was doing poorly in her science courses. Now an adviser had suggested she might not be a competitive candidate for medical school. She told me she was heartbroken. She said, "I just keep picturing myself in one of those doctor chairs behind a desk, talking to someone who has gotten a terrible diagnosis or who is facing a big change in life. I know I could be the kind of doctor people wish for in those situations, who can talk to the whole person, not just the patient."

I could feel how unhappy Sheila felt, but I found I kept thinking about her sitting in that chair behind the big desk. What was happening in the story in her head? I asked her: Do you always see yourself in the consulting room, the one with the wide desk, sitting in a comfortable chair? Is it never in the examining room, standing beside a patient who wears a gown and sits on an examining table?

Sheila gave me a strange look. Didn't I hear how unhappy she was? I said: Wait. Maybe you're unhappy because you're auditioning for the wrong role. In this community—that is, in our country—if you want to be the person who talks about the bigger life issues around medical diagnoses, you don't necessarily need a medical degree. You could be there as a clinical psychologist or a social worker. Maybe failing your science courses means that you shouldn't be a scientist. What if you set yourself a new, nonmedical career target and tried again? What if the problem isn't your science grades, but your dominant logic, which is telling you that you have to be a doctor when that's not the right role for you?

To sum up, when you need to break out of the dominant logic holding your innovation back, reconsider the story you're telling yourself with the help of the of the Russian nesting dolls.

- What is happening at the universal level—the *setting* of the story?
- What characters are in the story, and what other *characters* might be available? In particular, what other roles might you and others in the story be able to play?
- What other actions might you and the other characters take, and in what order?

chapter thirty

―――

THINK IN TERMS OF CYCLES, NOT LINES

Once a year or so, Rhonda would take out her guitar. She had played all the time when she was young, writing folk songs, performing for friends, and dreaming of a life as a singer-songwriter. Yet she had always held back, afraid she wasn't talented or pretty enough to succeed. Then life sped up. She got a demanding job, married, and had kids. As they grew, she took them to their music lessons and remembered how much she loved to play guitar. But now years had gone by, and she was older and still unsure how much talent she had. She took out her guitar, played a little, but it wasn't simple or easy. She didn't want to play all the same songs she had played as a teenager. She wanted songs that spoke to her as she lived now. She put her guitar away and then somehow another year would go by. She still thought about playing, even dreamed about it sometimes, but was singing songs even right for her anymore?

One thing that the passing of time had given her was insight. Rhonda could see now that her expectation of herself as a great talent, a star, had become a trap that kept her from playing and performing at all. She wanted to find a way to have music and performance in her life again. She took out her guitar and played with pleasure for a couple of hours, but then the old worries started again.

She had lost so much time! Was there room in the music industry for a mom nearing forty? Maybe music was just a youthful enthusiasm that couldn't satisfy her anymore anyway. Should she just sell her guitar on eBay and forget about it?

My advice to Rhonda was to stop trying to figure out the future in her head—that was almost impossible anyway—and instead focus on innovating a place for music in the life she had now. Her goal was clear, so rather than thinking in general about what might have been and what might or might not still be, I told her to pick targets. That guitar still called to her. How could she answer the call in specific, feasible ways that would feel like a "wow"?

She wanted to perform again, she told me, but she wasn't ready. Her playing was so rusty! And what songs would she play, anyway? She wasn't a young woman, after all. I said: Wait. You're saying great things. That's a target right there. Could you commit to perform again, once? Rhonda's thoughts leapt ahead into the future. She asked me: What if my playing is a mess? What if I make a fool of myself in public? What if I can't come up with a full set list? What if I don't even love playing the way I used to?

I said: Good, yes, those are fine questions, but don't answer them with *thinking*. There's no data on the future. Answer your questions with experiments. What if you could get one song ready and perform it at an open-mike night? Rhonda's eyes lit up. She said: I'd need to have a few songs—three songs, so I could pick the one that felt right in the moment, like I used to do. And I'd need to try them out somewhere safe to begin with.

As we talked it over together, Rhonda set these targets: She would choose and rehearse three songs she used to play—there had to be a few that still felt right to her, even though she wasn't nineteen anymore. In two weeks, she'd sing those three songs at home for a friend who was also a musician. Maybe she wouldn't be able to play anymore. Maybe she'd hate performing. But she would give it a try.

Two weeks later, she played for the musician friend and her kids. Then she asked them to join her for a "review." Had she enjoyed herself? No one had a doubt about that. Was her playing good enough for a friendly gathering? Definitely. Was this something she wanted to do again? Yes.

Encouraged, Rhonda set a new round of targets. She would learn two more songs in the next two weeks. She would do a test performance of the five songs for her musician friend, using him as her "expert" to refine her performance and help select one song as her best one so far. And if they agreed she was ready to perform, she would take her first practical shot on goal: She would commit to attending the open-mike night at a local café, where anyone could sign up on a list and take the stage for five minutes. She would invite only a few trusted friends and her kids.

Waiting at the open-mike night, Rhonda shook with nervousness, but once she got onstage she was fine. She loved performing for a real audience again, and she enjoyed hearing some of the other participants. She stayed late at the café, talking with two other folk singers she had met. They had been doing this longer than she had, and they knew more about the practical side of being a performer in her area. It was difficult to get a solo gig in town, but what if the three of them offered themselves as a group act? If each of them could get ten people to attend, that might be enough to convince the café to make them the featured performers on a weeknight. Now, of course, Rhonda would need more than one song.

one step closer

Rhonda still did not know if she was meant to be a folk singer or how much success she could achieve. But now that mattered less. She was riding the cycles of innovation, each set of experiments leading her to set new targets, seek new expertise, make new attempts, and review the results in terms of their practical value for her next attempts. She had begun to expect innovation to move not in a short, quick line ending in ultimate success or failure, but in a series of cycles, each one making her a little wiser, a little more confident, and a little clearer on her specific goals.

She had also discovered that it wasn't necessary to see the whole journey in a moment. She didn't have to know if music was going to be her second career. She didn't have to know where she would be a year from now. For the time being, it was enough that she was making music every day and looking forward to another performance. All that was necessary, as she ran each new set of experiments, was to get one step closer.

The experiments that moved her forward step-by-step were often rough improvisations. She made use of whatever was handy in the way of materials and advice—some old songs, a new song she heard on the radio, the support of her kids, and the experience of the other performers she met at her first open-mike night. She was reminded of MacGyver, the television secret agent who solved difficult technical problems with whatever materials he could find nearby—duct tape, chewing gum, what have you. Each solution not only got him out of his current jam, it also made him a little smarter, strengthening his powers of innovation for the next cycle. Rhonda realized that the innovation she had created was not just three performance-ready songs or five minutes in front of an audience on a certain Tuesday night; the real innovation was to learn how to be what she had wanted to be. Through her experiments and reflections she was finding a personal strategy—the unique method that would work for Rhonda. As she moved through innovation's cycles, a new capability was emerging in her.

I say cycles, not circles, because when we innovate mindfully, setting smart targets and reviewing and revising as we go, we don't wind up where we began. The shape this cyclical movement draws is not a circle but a spiral, like a road that winds repeatedly around a mountain as it climbs to the top, or like an airplane circling as it ascends, climbing higher each time around until it reaches cruising altitude—and then can complete its journey. Each time around the cycle, each set of experiments, is a part of the journey.

step IV

SEE THE WHOLE JOURNEY

To be interested in the changing seasons is a happier state
of mind than to be hopelessly in love with spring.
—George Santayana

Let me tell you the story of Almost-Clever Mike. Mike was a successful businessman who *almost* managed to dodge the Great Recession. Smart and attentive, a great creativizer, he watched the weather and he noticed increasing numbers of worried articles in the more thoughtful newspaper and magazines about the real estate market being overvalued. He talked to the people around him and he heard, over and over, that he was a fool not to put his money into real estate. People who knew little about business, including his sister, a clarinetist in the local symphony orchestra, made fun of him. Real estate was a sure bet, he was told repeatedly. But Mike was clever enough to remember that no investment is a sure bet, and to wonder at the rampant casino mentality among casual investors. He was clever enough to sense that the weather was about to change. And he was self-authorizing enough to shift his approach to his personal finance when no one else was doing so. Switching from Compete to Control, he gave up the goal of having as profitable a year as possible and set out to protect what he had from the coming storm. He took all his money out of the stock market and real estate (except for his own home) and put it into gold and treasuries and cash.

Then the storm hit. Mike wasn't making a lot of money from his investments but he was safe from the massive losses all around him. He felt pretty good about himself. Privately, he celebrated. Then, about three months into the recession, Mike got a phone call from his sister. She and his brother-in-law were wiped out. They were going to lose their home. Could he help?

Mike was furious, but what is a brother to do? He wrote a check and got the house out of receivership. Then a couple of months later, Mike got a call from his goddaughter. She was afraid she had to drop out of college. She had parked her tuition savings money in the market, but now more than half of it was gone. So Mike wrote another check. Then he gave his parents a call to see how their retirement accounts were faring.

In the end, Mike didn't dodge the Great Recession at all. He took as big a hit as anyone he knew. Clever as he was, when he took shelter from the storm, he left one nesting doll outside in the rain: community. He had forgotten the nesting doll mantra: *Look up, down, and around.* Despite his insight into the universal level of market changes and despite his disciplined personal response, he had forgotten that he was connected to others still out in the storm—in this case, his family.

I don't mean to sound critical of Mike. This is probably the hardest single aspect of innovation: Every time you move through a cycle of innovation, even if that cycle is an amazing success, a fresh cycle begins and your situation changes. We must learn to see beyond any given goal and try to imagine what lies beyond. In Step IV, "See the Whole Journey," I show you how to broaden your focus from single innovations to the larger cycles of innovations that will carry you like turning wheels on the longer journeys of careers, relationships, businesses, and lives. How? By discovering that life moves as a series of innovations, and for that reason it follows the same predictable progression. Whether you want to know how an entrepreneurial start-up becomes a global powerhouse, how a religion spreads through the world, or how an individual thrives over the course of one or more careers, you will find that innovations always move in a reliable sequence. Individuals and organizations alike rotate through the same four approaches to value: Create, Compete, Collaborate, Control, and Create again, renewing the cycle. In Step IV, I'll show you how to make use of that cycle to make a successful and satisfying life.

chapter thirty-one

WELCOME CREATIVE DESTRUCTION

Over the years, in what you might call the personal innovation field, I've spoken with many people—mentors, business coaches, consultants, "personal excellence trainers," therapists, and so on. There are some good ones out there, but I'm sorry to say that what I've heard most often is a kind of cynicism. "Oh, sure," one consultant I won't name said not long ago, "when they hire you they say what they really want is innovation. They're ready to make the big changes to move forward! And they're all enthusiastic until you get down to work and then it's like, 'Wait—you don't expect us to *change* all of this, do you?'"

When I hear this kind of innovation cynicism, I half know what the cynic is talking about. Because it's true that as you move through the cycles of experimentation and review and further experimentation, learning from each review what works and what doesn't, and revising your thinking, your understanding and partnerships, you must change. And the more you have to change—or ask the people around you to change—the more you will encounter resistance. The cynics are absolutely right that the would-be innovators who sail smoothly to sea, enthusiastic to try something new, inevitably hit rougher weather, resistance, and even a strong desire on the part of the crew to turn the ship around and go home.

Why does this happen? Some people will tell you it's because people are liars—they enjoy hiring someone to talk about becoming new and improved, but they won't do the work. On the other side, the ever-hopeful fans of psychological-type indicators will tell you it's just a matter of style—when I begin to innovate, I'm changing the style the people around me have come to expect, and now we have a clash of personal styles. But if we learn to understand and work sensitively with each other's styles, we'll discover that underneath the surface differences of style we all want the same things and we can get along.

It would be nice if that were the case, but it's not. The conflict that is natural to innovation isn't just a matter of style. We all want different things, and the reason we want different things is not just because we have different styles. We want different things because we are trying to go in different directions. If you and I want to live together, and I like a quiet house in the country and you like an apartment in the middle of downtown nightlife, the issue is not style. The issue is that we want to live in different ways. Doing it my way destroys your chance to have what you want and doing it your way destroys mine.

These tensions are obvious in a corporate setting—the new-product development people, with their green or Create approach, usually hate the manufacturing people, with their red or Control approach. The more a company devotes its resources to making products as efficiently as possible, the fewer resources are left over for inventing new ones. Typically, if one of those two groups gets to fund its plans, hit its targets, and take home nice big bonuses at the end of the year, then the other group won't. Recall the quote by the visionary innovator Marshall McLuhan, who said that innovation not only enhances something, it also destroys something else. That's not a mistake or a mismanagement of personal styles. That's what innovation does. The cassette tape killed the 8-track tape. The MP3 file nearly killed the entire music business. This is why businesspeople refer to big innovations as "category killers." And it's why we called our model *Competing* Values: Innovation is not just a meeting of varied styles, it's a competition, and competitions typically end with winners and losers.

As far as that goes, the innovation cynics are right. Whenever you try to nurture innovation, whether in a nation or in your morning routine or in anything in between, you are challenging the established division of resources: If you want to do things a new way, even if it's an improvement, there will be someone (or some part of you) who stands to lose because you're taking resources away from those who do things the old way. Ask a family systems therapist what happens when a family member gathers the clan and says, "We have to be honest: Dad is an alcoholic, and if he goes on this way, he's going to die." Do the other family members praise the truth-teller for bravery and honesty? Not usually. Usually, they call the person an ingrate and act as if the only problem is the terrible way that person talks about Dad. They shoot the messenger.

Jonas Salk, who invented the cure for polio, famously said that if you do work that contradicts prevailing ideas, the response from the establishment comes in three stages. First, they say you're wrong. If you keep going, they say you're immoral. And if you still keep going, then they take credit for your work. That's why I tell innovators who tell me they're hitting resistance: Well, sure! What did you expect? You say members of the organization are suddenly being mean to you. You're the one traumatizing them! You're the one encouraging the sailors to leave the safe, comfortable harbor and expose the ship to ocean waves and storms and, who knows, maybe even sea monsters. If they mutiny sometimes, it's not because they're crazy.

Every innovation pushes some older approach out. Every innovation takes someone's lunch money. If you push hard enough, the other force will fight back. Those fighting back are not evil; they are defending something: religion, morality, their paycheck. Unless you want a fight with them, it is necessary to take their concerns

seriously. The Welker family discovered this when they tried to settle the estate of Harold Welker, the oldest brother in the family and
a devoted fisherman. He left behind a large collection of fly-fishing
baits, including some valuable antiques dating back to the 1930s. His
two younger brothers, also fishermen, split the collection between
them, keeping some baits to fish with and selling the rest to collec-
tors. They assumed that his daughter, Darlene, would have no interest in the baits because she didn't fish. Darlene didn't want the baits
either for fishing or as antiques, but she was outraged that the brothers had broken up the collection. To them, it had a Compete meaning: It was a means to catch more fish and make some money. To
her, it had a Collaborate meaning: It was the physical sign of her
father, and she wanted to be able to look at it now and then because
it brought back memories.

The uncles assumed that if Darlene had wanted some of the
baits, she would have asked for them. Darlene assumed that the uncles' unilateral action showed disrespect for her father and for her.
She stopped speaking to them. The extended family, which had been
close, stopped socializing together. The uncles' use of the baits
pushed out Darlene's use, and their inability to acknowledge her
sense of value had a terrible cost for what had been a close clan.

Innovation by its nature operates through what the economist
Joseph Schumpeter called "creative destruction." It's true of smaller
innovations, too. Say a dad comes home from work one day with a
great new idea for a family vacation: Instead of renting that cottage
by the beach as usual, that cottage the family can't quite afford this
year (and that the dad was finding a little boring anyway), why don't
they drive across the country together, camping out and seeing the
beauty and history of America up close? The day that Dad has the
idea, he comes home feeling like a genius: It will be something new,
something that brings the family together. It will be less expensive,
more educational, and more of an adventure.

He makes his announcement and looks around. Everyone seems

unhappy. Everyone has a different way to say no. To his son, vacation means skimboarding and boogie-boarding at the beach. How is he going to do that at a campsite? To his daughter, a vacation means hanging out with her summer friends whom she only sees when she's at the cottage. How's she going to do that if she's stuck with her family halfway across the country? The siblings don't agree on much these days, but right off they agree on one thing about this plan: "Educational" sounds way too much like school. Even Mom is looking glum: Camping sounds like it means a whole lot of unpacking and repacking, not to mention awkward cooking over fires and washing clothes in Laundromats. Is it an adventure her husband is proposing or a menial summer job?

You can see the trouble. Dad's innovation threatens to destroy what everyone else in the family valued about their pre-innovation vacation. But destruction is not always a bad thing. If you consider any of the examples of innovation in this book, you'll see that Marshall McLuhan was right, and every enhancement also involved some destruction. Dan had to shut down his struggling traditional karate dojo before he could open his more child-friendly success. Aruna had to quit her old law job before she could establish her new arts-oriented practice. Mike had to sell all of his bull market investments before he could buy the bear market investments that would have allowed him to ride out the collapse of real estate, were it not for the needs to his family. As Joseph Schumpeter wrote: "Out of destruction a new spirit of creativity arises."

The secret to finding that new spirit of creativity is to welcome diversity, by which I mean to look for the ways that doing something differently might actually be an improvement for everyone. This is a different idea of diversity than the buzzword we often hear. I am not using "diversity" to mean that deep down we're all the same, so we should just play nice and get along. What I mean is that we have real differences, and every choice among differences is a trade-off with costs, but the best arrangement for reaching our shared goals probably involves using a variety of elements. When opposition arises to innovation, as it always will, the goal is to turn that opposition into an effective hybrid. Growth is born from the tension and constructive conflict of opposing forces. Aruna scaled back her Compete approach but didn't give it up completely: She may have become a lawyer for artists, but she was still a lawyer. Dan scaled back his traditional Control approach to make room for more Collaborate, but he was still demanding and strict when it came to the criteria for moving up a level and getting the next color belt.

We're not all just the same. We really are different, and that gives us different gifts and ideas that can lead to new and powerful hybrids. The secret to creative destruction is to let everyone bring their ideas and let the ideas compete. Lasting success comes not from one approach driving another off its territory or from an even compromise; it comes from the willingness to do something new to get the job done better. As Ringo Starr said of the Beatles, what made the band so great was that whether a musical idea came from the band member who wrote the song, another band member, the producer, friends and family, or anyone else who happened to be around, the group picked the one that served the song best. The effective hybrid benefits everyone involved, no matter what percentage of the innovation came from any one contributor: A rising tide lifts all boats.

Coming back to the family disagreeing about what vacation to take, there are only two ways they will go with Dad's new idea. One is if the dad strong-arms the rest of them into it, which will limit them to his ideas, rather than combining the best ideas of the group. It will also create tension and unhappiness that will hover over the entire trip. The other way is if all of them bring their concerns and their creativity and they hash it out together. Are there cool things to do on this trip, even if there won't be much boogie-boarding? Are there other cool people to meet besides the usual summer friends? Is there time for the daughter to stay with a summer friend before the camping trip starts? Are there ways to address Mom's concerns, so the trip is a vacation for all? Maybe there is a part of the country that everyone has wanted to see. Maybe the kids can each bring a friend and the trip will include a couple of campsites near beaches, but the kids have to do the cooking and cleaning. Somewhere in the diversity and disagreement is the potential for a more satisfying family vacation than anyone in the family has taken before.

The resistance and conflicts we encounter in innovation are unavoidable, but they're also predictable. Whatever innovation approaches that you want to take, you will get resistance from the opposite approaches. I personally prefer to innovate as a Compete and a Create, and so my blue and green plans regularly encounter resistance from the other side. Controls say, Wait, Jeff, I don't think this blue system of yours is going to function properly, and if it doesn't we're all going to look like fools. Collaborates say, We like where you're going but, whoa, Jeff, do you have to be so hard on people? These folks will fight me to protect their turf, but they will also have good ideas that I have missed. So my best chance to see my innovations completed will be to welcome innovative diversity and to make room for exactly those reds and yellows I might at first prefer to ignore.

the cycle of innovation

How do I do that? Over the years, I've come to rely on two mentors, each one very different in temperament and strengths. One of them is the former CEO of a top multinational corporation, the most thoughtful and analytical man you'll ever meet. He's also contemplative, extremely loyal, and quite reserved. A lot of people do not naturally assume that we are friends, let alone that we have a bond that is as important as anything in our work lives. I come to him fired up about my new Create ideas and plans and he says nothing. He never gives me a quick response or a snap decision. But he gets back to me three weeks later with an incredibly detailed response. Even more than my academic colleagues at other schools, he knows how to improve my research and he can explain his critiques in precise detail. In a sense, we are in conflict all the time. When we talk about my work, his full effort goes into telling me where I've skipped steps, made too many assumptions, or created a system that won't function in the long run. I listen to him because I understand that this is where I am weak and he is strong. His insights have saved me from several of the biggest mistakes I could have made in my career—mistakes I didn't make, thanks to him.

What he has wanted, which most people never guess, is to be helpful, to pass on the deep and meaningful things he's learned over his career. Meanwhile, students are always knocking on my innovation lab door, looking for guidance. So I've been able to connect him to young people who want help, and this has added a missing dimension to his life. He provides the red I'm missing, making sure my creative ideas are under good enough control, and I provide some of the yellow, the access to the student community, involving him in more collaborative activities.

Seeking a diverse range of guidance is not the only way to welcome creative destruction. It's just as important to learn to respect that each approach to innovation has to operate in its own ways. Let me give an example. I've known many people who have succeeded at work with a Control approach, but who yearn inside to be more creative. Often these are people who took the lower-risk, higher-reward career track but still wish to cook gourmet food or photograph nature or sew their own clothes—whatever it is their inner artisan feels called to do. I've seen many of these people who are good at scheduling tasks and completing them take the same approach to their neglected green sides. And so I hear things like, "For my New Year's resolution, I'm going to write poetry from six thirty to seven thirty every morning before work." But can they actually write poetry early in the morning? Many creative people I've known have times of the day that are by far their most productive. I know one screen-writer who can get more writing done between about ten at night and one in the morning than in the entire length of a regular work-day. His "create" work has to get done in a Create way. He can't force it into a Control straitjacket of efficient scheduling.

Of course, if he works late into the night, that will put pressure on his morning routine, and perhaps on his whole workday. He's going to be more tired the next day. His new Create approach is going to feel like a threat to his established Control routine. Is it worth it? An innovator's answer would be: Experiment. Try setting the alarm early and discover what results you get. Then try working at night and see how that experiment goes. Maybe writing times will have to be Thursday, Friday, and Saturday nights from ten to eleven thirty, and Fridays at work he'll have to drink more coffee. The key is that he tolerates some creative destruction in his own life.

I can't stress this enough. Tolerating creating destruction is the only road to ongoing success because it allows you to continue on the journey, and the journey will always move through the cycle of Collaborate, Create, Compete, and Control. When I started my academic career as a junior professor of business, I had no publications, no reputation, and no business clients. I had to distinguish myself somehow, to make myself unique, so like a start-up business or an aspiring artist, I had no choice but to act as a Create. I experimented like crazy with how to convey what I knew about innovation to business students. I played guitar for my classes. I invited a master violin maker to talk about excellence in craftsmanship. To help students get into the "flow" state of creativity, I required them to get a massage and to learn to meditate. In these ways, they practiced removing the physical and mental tension that can prevent us from hearing ourselves think. I offered a formal course on creativity in business, which had never been done and was widely considered impossible to do, back then.

Among my many green experiments, I had many failures. I came in for all kinds of doubt and criticism from more senior professors. But I also found that some of my experiments proved to be good ideas that gained traction. As I established myself, I was able to launch my lab and attract business clients. Now that I had a functioning business, I had a company to grow. We had all the practical challenges of any competitive venture: finding new clients, hiring new staff, making payroll every two weeks. I was still as creative a person as I had been a few years before, but I had to change my approach and think primarily like a CEO, not like an artist or an academic iconoclast. I had to make sure the business thrived. I had to live as a Compete.

Yet the more the company thrived, the more it outgrew my personal reach. That meant I had to use my Collaborate skills to hire others to do increasing amounts of the work and still maintain the quality. I had to partner with others in my community and grow my business by working on my connections.

Then, as my business grew even more, I had to think about systems and processes to make us more efficient, reliable, and productive. That meant acting as a Control, standardizing processes to eliminate mistakes and waste. Growth was still important, but we were big enough that preserving what we already had mattered more than any single opportunity for new growth or any new innovation we might make. Again, I had to change my approach as the business matured. I had less and less time to be reflective or to try radical new approaches.

Finally, I began to realize that I would not be running this business forever. What would I leave behind? How could I create a legacy? Should I sell the business? Should I try to merge with a larger company? As my focus shifted increasingly to the transition out of this time in my life, I had to ask myself: What am I going to do *now*? And I felt the familiar challenge of tolerating creative destruction.

chapter thirty-two

WATCH FOR THE OFF-RAMPS
AND ON-RAMPS

When you ride with a student driver on the highway, you may be reminded of something that confident drivers forget: Piloting a car in a straight line at the same speed as the other cars is pretty easy, but slowing down to switch lanes and exit is actually a lot more challenging, especially if the driver doesn't know the route and is also checking a GPS readout or a map. Those off-ramp and on-ramp moments are where an inexperienced driver is likely to get into trouble—missing a turn, even getting into an accident—but those challenging moments are unavoidable. You can't stay on the highway forever. Similarly, when it comes to the journey of innovation, it's necessary to exit from one road to another. Creative dreams and ideas become competitive projects. Competitive projects require yellow partnerships to keep growing, and increasingly complex ventures need formal controls to keep them running smoothly. But these bigger, better-controlled ventures will be unable to make room for all of the green dreams and ideas of the people who work for them, and then the cycle must start again. In our highway analogy, that means it's necessary not only to get off the big superhighway but to do so while beginning a new trip that hasn't yet been thoroughly mapped. That's the most confusing part of the trip, the switch from the end of one leg of the journey to the beginning of another—the point where you can easily get lost, or worse, if you aren't watching out for the off-ramps and on-ramps.

Jake's success running a company that built recording studios and performance spaces brought him to the attention of his church, which wanted to renovate its basement meeting space to improve the acoustics and upgrade the technology so it could be used for musical and theatrical performances. Jake was an active churchgoer and he made time in his busy schedule to attend meetings of the design, planning, and finance committees. He brought church representatives to see the other auditoriums and studios he had built. He solicited bids among the contractors he knew for the church's job and oversaw the progress on the work. Over time, he guided the church through a very successful renovation, taking only enough payment to cover his expenses. As a result, he was asked to become even more involved in the church's plans, which included renovating its primary space and fund-raising for their long-term capital campaign. Jake was happy to help out an organization that was important to him, but he also saw how each success bred new projects with new requests, and the idea of that exhausted him. He realized that he needed to find an off-ramp.

In other words, Jake was at the end of an innovation cycle. Like the founder of a successful business who now sees his organization growing beyond his skills and interests, or like a film director who has completed the final cut, or like a stay-at-home parent whose kids are now entering school, freeing up time for other interests and goals, Jake needed to look for the off-ramp to take him off his present highway and the on-ramps available for the next stage of his journey.

At moments like these, we need to think around the colors to reconsider our role. Up till now, Jake had been the go-to "blue" for the church: He knew how to do successful sound- and performance-related construction projects, and he brought first a businesslike Compete approach to meeting the church's needs. Now he wanted to get out of that role and shift to a more yellow or Collaborate position, nurturing a group within the church that could do the work he had done rather than doing it himself. Yet he found that he kept getting drawn back into supervising the volunteers who were supposed to take his place.

How do you to find the off-ramps after you reach your innovation goals? There are four rules to remember.

1. *Cast an understudy.* Find someone who wants to learn to do what you are no longer interested in doing. Let that person fill in occasionally when you can't perform your accustomed role. In some cases, as often happens in business, if the understudy rises to the challenge, you might groom that person to be your replacement in the organization, freeing you to move on to other opportunities. In other cases, such as the stay-at-home parent who is now ready to leave the house a bit more, the understudy might be a babysitter who is only ever going to be a backup, but whose occasional "performances" are essential if the star is going to have time for other roles. Jake worked to find other church members who were interested not just in helping the church but in gaining experience for themselves in the kinds of work Jake did.

2. *Define your new role.* Jake didn't want to quit his involvement with the church, but he did want to limit the amount of time he put in, especially the amount of time he spent on tasks another church member could do. He made it clear that while he would no longer attend design, planning, or finance meetings, he would still make himself available to talk with the church leaders and to review the plans and assignments of responsibilities that were being made. In his church life, Jake was shifting from a Compete approach to a Collaborate approach, giving up being the project leader to become a trusted adviser.

3. *Look for new kinds of satisfaction.* Jake came to realize that with this change, he would no longer have the pleasure of running the

project and watching work go according to his plan. But he could still feel good that the church's needs were being met and that his experience was valued. Like a parent who'd seen his children off to sleepaway camp, he would miss the day-to-day closeness, but he knew his "children" were having a good time under a watchful eye, even though he wasn't there with them.

4. *Get outside support for your new role.* When you're driving down the highway, the easiest choice is always to keep going straight. Planning a new route and making sure to take the correct exit when it comes is more of a challenge, and sometimes we all need a navigator to assist us or a friend to talk to and keep us awake. There is always a voice for continuing on in a straight line forever, like the voice we're all increasingly likely to hear when we are about to go on vacation, asking: Couldn't you bring just a little work with you? Aren't you serious about your work? Jake imagined this wouldn't be a problem for him because his business required him to move among different projects, but he found that at the church it was harder not to get involved in supervising the people who had taken on his former roles, who were volunteers and relatively inexperienced.

One day, he spoke with another of the church's "trusted advisers," someone who had given a lot of time and hands-on effort but who since then had given up her intensive, day-to-day involvement with church projects. He asked her to give him some pointers. They began to meet every month or so to talk about how they could be of help to the organization—without being drawn back into their old, time-intensive roles.

In the same way, I've seen many caregivers—stay-at-home parents or grandparents, or adult children caring for aging parents—who find they struggle to work on other projects even when they do finally have more time. Years of shaping oneself as a Collaborate, available whenever and however you are needed, can be hard to shake off. Often we need someone else to speak up, consistently, for the outside commitment, someone riding alongside us to say: Look!

That's your exit! For a longtime caregiver, that might mean a friend or a personal trainer who calls and says, "I didn't see you at the gym last week. Are you coming today?" It might mean a creative "buddy" or a personal coach you meet with once a week, to review your progress on the creative project or business plan that got sidelined. Consider what sort of "navigator" you could use in the seat beside you, and find someone who can commit to being that voice for the new effort.

chapter thirty-three

WE ALL HATE CHANGE

I have a confession to make. There is an aspect of innovation that I've been soft-pedaling. The emotional challenge of innovation is more difficult than I've acknowledged, and the fact is that if you don't meet that emotional challenge, you will never get through the innovation cycles that lead you to satisfaction and success. So before I go any further, I have to stop and tell you my own sad story, a story of personal trial in the face of change: the lonesome ballad of the red recliner.

Now, I don't know about you, but I held on to a certain piece of furniture from my youth long after anyone might have expected me to keep it, that is, in my case, a pre-marriage piece of furniture. I did my doctorate at the University of Wisconsin, so my piece of furniture was bright red—Wisconsin Badgers red—and it was a recliner. This is where I sat to scream at the football game, and in my heart I knew that if I was sitting in my red recliner, the coach could hear me. In that recliner, I rocked my babies to sleep with the dog sitting next to me. It was not just a chair. It was the emotional center of my universe.

Then one day, my wife, whom I adore, said that she wanted to redecorate the house. She had a vision: Our house was going to be like a French bistro. She had names for the colors she wanted, names

I had never used, like "mustard yellow." I started hearing about "French blue." I didn't know what French blue was, but here was my beloved wife, sharing with me a Great Vision of Redecoration. What could I say? I said, "Yes, that sounds great. That would be a wonderful thing for the house to have." It never occurred to me that the Great Vision did not include the red recliner.

One night I came home late. I went to sit in my recliner, but there was no recliner. I searched the darkened house. And then I went down to the damp, dark, musty basement and there sat my lonesome, red recliner. Now I understood. It hadn't made the cut. It had no place in the great French bistro to come. But all right, all right, maybe I had a new vision for my red recliner. When I was a boy, hadn't I always loved a play fort? So I went out the next day. My mind was feverish. I bought the biggest television I could possibly fit into the basement. And I put it where? In front of the red recliner. I bought one of those videogames that makes the kids all jump up and down, where they can surf and play tennis and do almost anything you can think of, virtually, and I put that by the red recliner. Then I collected all the junky furniture that nobody used and put it around the red recliner. And now I had my basement fort.

Then about a month before Christmas, my red recliner went missing. There was a hole now in my fort in the basement. And sure enough, when Christmas came, under the tree Santa had brought back my recliner. But it was no longer red. Now it was covered with a fabric of French chickens in mustard yellow and French blue.

Why do I tell this story? Because it's a story about the emotional challenge of change, a change I could have seen coming but that I refused to see or accept. Even though I know perfectly well, in the abstract, that every innovation both makes something new and destroys something older, I still hate change. So do you. How do I know? Because everyone hates change, except for a few thrill-seekers and nutcases. How can I be deep into a book on innovation and only now say that I hate change? Because innovation isn't change.

Innovation inspires because innovation means growing toward something new, something better. But change is moving away from things and cutting them out. That might sound like a minor distinction, but think about the times you've had to give up something that was an important part of your life—even something as apparently ridiculous as an ex–graduate student's ancient reclining chair—and walk away. Not walk toward anything, just away. Many of the worst experiences in life fall into this category: giving up smoking or other addictions; leaving a relationship with no future; accepting a loved one's death. There is nothing innovative about it, nothing new or improved or more. Change is only less.

As you move around the cycle of innovation, from Create to Compete to Collaborate to Control, you step from innovation to innovation: It is possible to improve at every step. But when it is time to quit what you have been innovating and come back to create once again, whether you have failed or succeeded, you're going to have to walk away from something. Whatever you have tried to do has been done; now you need to find a new project. You have reached the point of change. In order to create something new, you will have to destroy at least part of your existing relationship to the innovation you have worked so hard to build, and that emotional challenge can derail your entire life.

The organizational consultant William Bridges makes a helpful distinction between change and transition. Change is what happens outside of you: a new project, a new boss, a new role in your life (or the loss of a role you cherished). Change is what makes you walk away. Transition is what happens inside of you, the process of coming to terms with change. Bridges observed that a transition moves in stages. It begins with denial, hurt, shock, fear—the very emotions I was feeling down in my basement, when it felt as if the loss of my red recliner meant the loss of my own emotional center.

During the Great Recession, I got at least a hundred calls from shocked, angry, confused people that went something like this: "Jeff, you're not going to believe this. I just got a pink slip. Jeff, this can't be happening. How am I supposed to make my house payments? What if we have to leave our school district? What is my wife going to say? This can't be happening." That's the voice of endings. That's the voice of the first stage of the transition.

It feels worse before it feels better. On the downward slope, those emotions are followed by anger, frustration, confusion, and stress—a period of chaos and disorientation in which we feel we don't know who or where we are. It is a time with great possibility for creative transformation, but also a time we are at risk of making bad decisions, including the decision to give up. In that place of chaos, some addicts attempt suicide; some angry lovers commit violent acts that change lives forever. But even in less melodramatic situations, in the period of chaos we may forget that the darkest hour is right before the dawn.

If we can weather the storm of chaos, the next phase brings increasing acceptance, understanding, and testing of new possibilities. In the recession, when I'd call to check up on someone after a while, I'd often be relieved to hear something like: "You know, I might be onto something. There's an opportunity out of state—I'm not sure yet that it works financially but I've always wanted to do something more meaningful/creative in a different part of the country." Some of the couples would have split up—maybe the relationship had been on life support for some time, and it took a financial shock to make that clear. Other couples would have discovered newfound strength and commitment as they weathered the hard times together. Gradually hope and optimism returned, and people were able to adapt to the change with growing confidence and enthusiasm. They had crossed over from an ending through the dangerous "neutral zone" and into a new beginning. They had made it through the transition.

Everyone goes through some version of these transitions when they reach a significant life change. Whether it's the student after graduation, the worker who has lost a job, or the founder of a business who has either sold the business or been forced out, the underlying emotional challenge is the same. The danger of the transition is that you will get stuck in the chaos or give up on your next innovation cycle before it even begins.

Personally, I'm a blue-green, so I tend to do a lot of planning of competitive strategies and creative responses. But in the stress of a transition, I may get stuck on a line of thinking I can't get off of. When that happens, I believe that I'm strategizing my way out of the problem when in fact I'm just wearing myself out. I spend time and energy preparing in detail for situations I've only invented in my head.

In *Innovation You* terms, one big risk during the bottom of a transition is that we slip into the negative zone, relying so heavily on the innovation approach that comforts us that we have no room for its opposite. Greens go so deep into the Create approach that they lose necessary practicality and control. Blues become so competitive they reject their yellow communities. And so on. So it's especially important in times of transition to keep checking in with those people and sources from other colors whom you rely on to give you a wider perspective. Keep lighting your fires where the sparks of diversity fly. Keep watching the weather. Don't hunker down alone with your intense feelings, imagining you're the only one who ever faced a difficult change. Remember that even if you have failed, the failure cycle is an inevitable part of innovation. Apple almost went bankrupt in the '90s before it could rule the world a decade later.

The people I knew who came through the recession with good mental health did so in part because they had the expectation that there would be a transition and it would take time. Much of the discomfort of time is that it's the expectation of time, not time itself, which makes people crazy. The people who could say to each other, "We're going to give this recession a couple of years to work itself out" were able to sleep at night because they remembered that the situation would not last forever.

The power of expectations is something they understand very well, actually, at Disney World. I hate to wait in a crowd—I'll leave a restaurant rather than wait for a table to clear—so I dreaded bringing my kids to Disney. But when I finally broke down and went, I discovered that they have clocks on the lines for the big rides that say, "Your wait for this ride is about X minutes." So I could say to my wife, Why don't you wait here and I'll take the kids to get a drink, look at stuffed animals, go to the bathroom, whatever it might be that could save me from standing and waiting in a crowd. Sometimes I answered some emails on my phone. For some people, the time between rides wouldn't be a significant transition, but for me it made all the difference to know that it was coming and about how long it might last.

There is no magic cure for the emotional challenge of transitions, but, like a weather report, knowing that the storm is coming can make it easier to recognize why you may feel so bad and to find people who can help you get through.

chapter thirty-four

─────

BUILD A PORTFOLIO LIFE

An old friend telephoned. I'll call him Bart. "Hey, buddy!" he said. "I've got great news!" But something in his tone made me nervous. We'd been close for a long time but these days we rarely spoke. I'd met Bart when we were both single; I'd gone to his wedding to his wife, Margie; I knew his children—the two they had planned for, both boys in high school now, and the twin girls who were unexpected. When the twins arrived, Bart and Margie welcomed them as a blessing, but for years afterward they struggled, professionally and personally. He hung on to a job that didn't fit him because they needed the paycheck. She told me once that when she was alone— which was rare—she hardly remembered who she was besides someone else's mother or wife. Their lives asked a lot of them. Recently, though, the twins had started going to school full-time. The most demanding years seemed to be ending.

"Buddy, listen!" he said now. "Something amazing has happened. After all these years, I've met my soul mate!"

My heart sank. There had been a time in my life, when I was younger, when friends would often call up to tell me about their new romances or their wedding plans. It was purely happy news. It made everything else in life sweeter. But that time was mostly past.

"Your soul mate?" I asked.

"I know it's kind of unexpected," my friend said. "But I think this is it. I feel so alive again. This gal at work—you have to meet her—this is the gal who was meant for me."

"Is she Margie's soul mate?" I asked.

"What?"

"You said that she's your soul mate. Is she your kids' soul mate?"

Bart was shocked. How could I speak to him this way when he finally had some good news? But to me, it didn't sound like good news. To me it sounded like the pressure had been building in his life for years as his habitual ways slowly stopped working for him, both at work and at home. He was like someone on the highway who sees the engine temperature readout on his dashboard climb up and the warning light turn red, but who feels he's in too much of a rush and he doesn't want problems, so he keeps driving until the engine blows. I didn't doubt that his life felt unfulfilling at times; I could imagine that he and Margie found their marriage a challenge. But the innovation he'd come up with was twenty years out-of-date.

Had he been single, finding the right partner, someone to inspire him and help him remake his life, might have been a great step. In fact, if I remembered correctly, that was how he and Margie got together, when he was stuck in a job that was all wrong for him and she helped him see that he was capable of more. Now he was grabbing for the one innovation that had worked before, but what works when you're thirty and single doesn't necessarily play the same way when you're fifty with a wife and a house full of kids.

no innovation lasts forever

Innovation is the only form of value that has a shelf life: Innovations go sour like milk. Think about when you buy Christmas presents. You're looking for the new thing, the gift that is fresh and charming. And next year, you will be doing it again, looking for a fresh and charming gift for the same person. The gift most likely to be wrong is the one you gave the year before. This year's great new gift will have become old stuff. It might even get recycled or thrown away. Innovation is a relative state—what's new and improved is only new and improved relative to the situation where something is used up or lacking.

Think about innovations in food. Back when there were only a few small local stores and people still hunted and fished for themselves (like my grandfather did), a supermarket was an amazing innovation. Now supermarkets are old hat, and there is an innovative movement to get back to local sourcing of food, which in my part of the country includes hunting your own deer and catching your own fish. As Marshall McLuhan put it in his third principle of innovation, innovations return us to something in our past, giving us an opportunity to recover what we have lost but still long for. This is why Barnes & Noble bookstores are designed to feel like the library at a college campus. And it's why I watch fishing programs on TV when I don't have time to steal away for an afternoon on a lake.

What does this have to do with my friend Bart? After years living in the Control position, putting all of his energy into maintaining the systems that kept money coming in and the family functioning, he was feeling the dissatisfaction that had gathered and the tremendous pressure that had built to satisfy the sides of him that had gotten neglected. But he had only one, outdated innovation in mind to try. I didn't doubt that he'd met a compelling woman. I just doubted that busting up his marriage and leaving his kids for this compelling woman were going to satisfy the deep need he felt for a better life.

Bart got angry at me for being hard on him, but I could easily have said worse: I could have pointed out, for example, that when he first told me about Margie, way back when, he'd used the exact same words: "This is the gal who was meant for me."

I've started this chapter with a melodramatic story, but I hear quieter versions of this story all the time. A senior vice president calls me up and says, "Jeff, I don't know what to do. I've built out most of what I can do in this company and, frankly, I'm bored." This is always someone who came in fired up to put some great new ideas to work, reshaping them in a Compete environment so that the ideas could bear fruit. Now, he's succeeded, which means he's done. The ideas have worked, the company has shifted to a Control approach to keep the profits coming, and now this person has to reinvent his or her life to find areas that need a Create approach again—or that person is likely to do something destructive.

I spoke in an earlier chapter about creative destruction. The truth is that when you reach the end of an innovation cycle, destruction is really the only choice. We're lucky that it comes in two flavors: reckless and creative. But creative destruction is still destructive. Even a creative artist as successful as Picasso famously said, "I am the great destroyer."

It might seem as if my approach to innovation has now run into a terribly thorny and impenetrable problem of human existence: I'm saying that we all will reach crossroads in our lives where the things we've always done don't work anymore, where nothing will seem to satisfy us and destruction will loom. Yet this is the same problem that investors face every time they consider how best to allocate their assets. What can seem bleak as a life situation—what hope is there for Bart and Margie?—is far more hopeful if we make a surprising analogy to an investment portfolio.

A balanced portfolio is usually described in terms of the percentages of resources the investor commits to each of four areas—areas that by now should seem familiar to you. Here's an example: If you meet with a good investment professional, she might suggest that you put half of your money in high-performing, relatively low-risk stocks such as General Electric, Procter & Gamble, and so forth—in other words, the blue or Compete quadrant, where the possibility of success is relatively high and the risk is relatively low. A total of 10 to 15 percent could go into more radical stuff—smaller, less tested companies with a higher potential for growth, such as domestic start-ups or foreign companies in developing markets. This is the green or Create quadrant, where you'll probably lose some of your investments but where there is also the potential for huge growth when you pick a winner.

You might also tell the investment adviser that there's some amount of your money—let's say 10 percent—that she can't touch, because you have plans for it that have no financial significance, but matter to you for other reasons—funding a scholarship for underprivileged kids at your old school or giving your aging uncle some extra money because you promised your father you'd look after him. That is the yellow or Collaborate quadrant, where the "payout" is not in dollars but in community.

Finally, you might be advised to keep the remaining 20 or 30 percent of your assets in cash or treasuries, something safe and handy because you never know what the future holds. Some of that money might also be going toward life and disability insurance. This is the red or Control quadrant, which keeps your whole system running even in the event of "errors"—loss of a job, downturn in the market, injury, illness, or death. Taken together, these allocations in each of the four quadrants are meant to balance your personal desires against the reality of changes in the larger world around you. That's the logic of an investment portfolio.

But as any asset-allocation-style investor knows, you can't just buy a bunch of investments and then forget about them. What happens, always, is that some of these investments perform better than expected and some perform worse. So let's say you have a great year in your high-risk "green" investments, but a relatively poor year in your moderate-risk "blue" investments. When you look at the value of each class of assets, you find that your greens have risen in value and now, instead of representing 15 percent, as you had planned, they are up to 20 percent. Meanwhile the blue ones that you determined should be half of your investments are down to 45 percent of your total holdings. To get back to the percentages you have allocated, it's necessary (in this example) to sell some from the green category and buy more of the blue.

Over time, as your personal situation changes, you would also change your target percentages to suit your changing desires and situation. For example, as you grew older, you would want a smaller percentage of long-term investments (green) and a higher percentage of short-term investments and ready cash (blue and red), because you are less likely to be around in the long term to enjoy the benefits of green investments.

No portfolio can ever be the final, perfect one. Success comes from understanding that portfolios require adjustments forever. For people who invest in the stock market, this is familiar, but what is not familiar is that this approach works just as well for the "investment" of our personal time, effort, and care. Green or Create "investments" have the power to disrupt the status quo—they are high risk—but if they pay off, they don't just put something new in your life, they can give you a whole new life. (The odds are extremely low, for example, that Alison, who took the summer off to dog-sit and design an app, will create the next killer app or game. But if she does create a blockbuster, that success will remake her entire life.) Blue or Compete "investments" pay off in less transformative but more reliable prosperity and health. Red or Control "investments" pay out like insurance, protecting you against failure, accidents, and unexpected challenges. Yellow or Collaborate "investments" don't so much pay off as pay it forward, bettering the community of which you are a part.

Bart's mistake was not that he "invested" so much of his time and energy in his unexpectedly large family. Nor was he wrong to look for more personal satisfaction when the very high demands of his family life began to let up. His mistake was to ignore the growing pressure in his life, a pressure that came from "investing" almost all of himself in the red or Control quadrant, so that he came to feel that there was nothing growing in his life and that he was slowly dying.

His portfolio was profoundly out of balance. Margie was also overin-vested, in yellow and red. Both had begun to feel as if they weren't whole people anymore. And both had something in common that they didn't recognize: They were neglecting a key part of the middle nesting doll. They had forgotten to nourish the community that was their marriage.

When the chance came to rebalance his portfolio, Bart lunged impulsively and blindly for a Create approach—New wife! New job! New life!—in the way that had worked for him once twenty years before. In the investment analogy, it was as if Bart had invested all of his family's savings in one new start-up computer company because twenty years before he had made a lot of money buying Apple. I can understand the emotional impulse, but that is a perfect example of rotten investing.

Of course, I understand that Bart wasn't making a conscious choice to become infatuated with a coworker. Feelings aren't thought-ful decisions, the way investments ought to be. We feel whatever we feel when we feel it. But the choices and commitments that we make based on our feelings can be made like investment decisions—and that is both our best hope for finding the new dreams that will give our lives purpose and vitality, and our best protection against fool-ishly blowing up what we have already built.

what's the next dream?

Bart and Margie forgot that their portfolio would have to keep changing. They were overwhelmed by the nature of babies: Like start-up businesses and cutting-edge artistic or scientific projects, babies make huge, sometimes overwhelming demands on us at first. As they grow older, they demand less of our time, and then finally, ready or not, they grow up, and we have to give our now-grown "babies" to the world. Every organization or project or creation in your life will either reach a natural end or in some way grow beyond you—and if it happens that a project does need you forever, the day will come when it will become too big and fast for you: You will no longer be able to keep up with it.

And so we must remember to ask: What about other babies? Or to put it in Competing Values terms: Where can we next take a Create approach? The end of something is never just a question of riding out a rough emotional transition. We need new commitments, other ways of "investing" not just our money but our time, our energy, our creativity, and our caring. What happens beyond this cycle? Where can we find a small amount of time and resources to take a green or Create approach again? Ask yourself, early and often: What's the next dream?

innovation for life

When you start thinking of your entire life as a portfolio of innovation "investments," you take a crucial step in becoming a lifelong innovator. You stop thinking of innovation as something you do in individual projects and shift to the overall journey. *Everything* you do this month can be seen in the terms we used in Step III: as a set of experiments that will bring you closer to or farther from your targets—and that need to be reviewed before you settle on your next set of experiments.

I often advise people to schedule time to rebalance their portfolios: Take an hour on the first Sunday of the month, for example. But the truth is that I do it whenever I feel the need. Whenever I feel that frustration building that means that my commitments are not getting me closer to what matters to me most, I take out my calendar and start thinking around the colors. I think of this as rebalancing my life portfolio.

exercise: check your life portfolio

Here is an exercise for visualizing your life portfolio to see whether it needs to be adjusted.

1. Use Figure 3 to take stock of your life portfolio. Select which of the eight goals of innovation are most important to you now. Enter your specific personal version of each goal. Along with "vitality," for example, you might write, "strengthen my knee until I can hike again" or "train for half-marathon." The goals are:

a. Collaborate:
   i. Capability: learning and skill development
   ii. Community: connection to family, friends, colleagues, or customers
b. Create:
   i. Creativity: new vision and creative expression
   ii. Discovery: psychological or spiritual insight
c. Compete:
   i. Vitality: physical health and mental focus
   ii. Prosperity: competitive effort to win financial well-being
d. Control:
   i. Security: safety, savings, and insurance
   ii. Productivity: consistent systems to sustain success

2. Note how much of your life you have given to each of these goals lately. You may wish to add up the hours spent on each over the last few weeks, but you might also find it's enough to estimate each as a percentage of your overall time, energy, and resources. In some cases it's enough just to note which areas received a lot, some, little, or none of your time and effort. Start out with a casual estimate and become more precise if that seems useful.

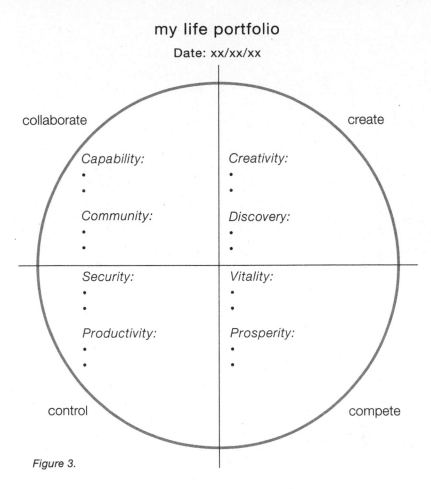

my life portfolio
Date: xx/xx/xx

collaborate

create

Capability:
*   •
*   •

Creativity:
*   •
*   •

Community:
*   •
*   •

Discovery:
*   •
*   •

Security:
*   •
*   •

Vitality:
*   •
*   •

Productivity:
*   •
*   •

Prosperity:
*   •
*   •

control

compete

Figure 3.

Before going further with the instructions for checking your life portfolio, let's return to the example from Step II, chapter 10, Caroline, the real estate agent who needed to care for her aging father. She was working hard to cut expenses and to care for him personally, but it was costing her too much to live that way. She had the possibility of more success selling summer homes, and she also had an idea for a new business she could start with her accountant, advising people in challenging financial straits. Figure 4 shows her life portfolio.

3. Are the time and effort you are giving each quadrant getting you what you hoped for? Holding each goal in mind, one at a time,

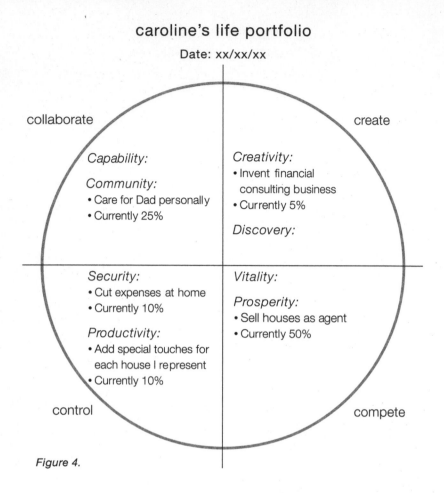

Figure 4.

conduct a quick after-action review, as you did in Step III. What worked? What didn't? Should you adjust the amount of time, energy, resources, and caring you give to each category? Enter the new percentages on your chart as "revised targets." Caroline, as we saw in chapter 11, decided to cut out her "create" commitments (now was not the time to develop a new business for the long term) and to cut down on the care she provided for her father, as well as some of the economies in her personal life that were taking a lot of her time. She came up with the following revised targets:

Invent consulting business—decrease from 5% to 0%.

Sell more houses as agent—increase from 50% to 75%.

Care for her father—decrease from 25% to 10% (pay for care facility).

Economize at home—10% (maintain).

Add special touches to her homes sold—decrease from 10% to 5%.

See Figure 5 for Caroline's revised target life portfolio.

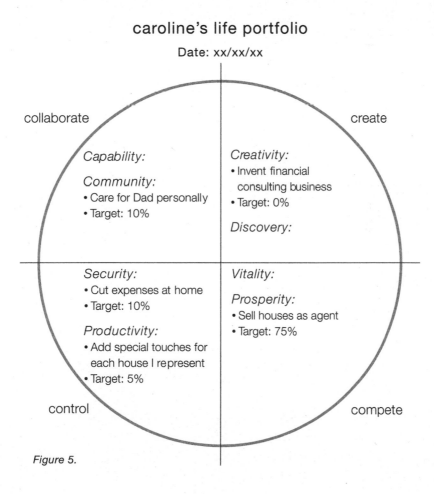

caroline's life portfolio

Date: xx/xx/xx

collaborate

create

Capability:

Community:
• Care for Dad personally
• Target: 10%

Creativity:
• Invent financial consulting business
• Target: 0%

Discovery:

Security:
• Cut expenses at home
• Target: 10%

Productivity:
• Add special touches for each house I represent
• Target: 5%

Vitality:

Prosperity:
• Sell houses as agent
• Target: 75%

control

compete

Figure 5.

4. On a separate piece of paper, list the individual experiments or attempts you made in the service of *each* goal. Now conduct a quick after-action review for each one. Looking ahead:

    a. What specific actions or techniques could you stop because they are not succeeding?

    b. What new ones could you start?

    c. What should you do more or differently?

    d. What should you do less?

    e. What should you keep the same?

5. Revise your life portfolio to show your new target. Take out your calendar. Look for existing appointments you can cancel and other opportunities to put your revised commitments into action.

6. Put a day and time on the calendar for your next portfolio review. Consider asking someone to join you for support.

chapter thirty-five

——

EXPECT RESISTANCE

As you try to live according to your revised portfolio—what I
think of as leading a portfolio life—you will discover two forces that
constantly pressure you to give up your thoughtful and heartfelt
commitments. The first is the natural momentum of your primary
commitment, whatever that may be. Whichever of the four areas
gets the best of your energy and effort will be the one most likely to
grow—and as it grows, it will ask more of you. The places you go in
the service of that commitment will be the places that surround you,
and because they are right there in front of you, they will insist on
their ever greater importance.

If your main commitment is to a political campaign, for example,
you will be surrounded by others who think that politics is the center of the world. They will talk to you about the campaign even
when you are taking a lunch break or out for a beer after a long day.
When you have successes, they will ask you to take on more responsibilities because you have proved yourself. When there is a failure,
they will ask you to work harder to get the campaign back on track.
The campaign may come to seem like the only thing in the world
that is real. But the same would hold true if your primary commitment were to a laboratory research project or breeding dogs or writing a symphony.

The second pressure comes from the blue or Compete quadrant. In the United States and other money-focused countries, there is constant pressure to commit more resources to the blue quadrant because that is where you will always find the faster, easier money. If you have a day job and plan to write a screenplay, every day there will be reminders that other people are giving more of their time and effort to the day job, and seeing results. The screenplay might change your life, but as a green or Create activity, it is by definition long-term and high-risk. Just like General Motors, which developed the first hybrid engine in the 1970s but didn't commit the resources to bring it to market successfully, our most ambitious long-term dreams are always getting threatened by the call of short-term rewards. Americans say they know the importance of keeping a rainy-day fund and of saving for the future, but it is hard to sit on cash that could bring home a flat-screen television or fund a vacation. Similarly, it is a great thing to save for a child's education, but children are more likely to clamor for Disney World.

Given these pressures, many of us find at times that we have overinvested in one of the four areas at the expense of the others. Our lives become like an old-fashioned playground merry-go-round that spins faster as it gains riders. You may want to slow it down, but then the others will ask, Don't you care about the merry-go-round? It gets harder to slow down, but if you let the momentum build too much, the only other choice is to throw yourself off.

how to compete with "compete"

How to push back? "Compete" or blue goals are hard to resist in part because they provide relatively quick, tangible rewards. One way to strengthen other goals is to make them feel more like Compete goals. Set due dates. Build mechanisms into your life that make reaching your non-blue goals as close to automatic as possible: If your dream is to go back to school or to take a summer off to volunteer building houses for those who can't afford them, each time you get paid have your bank automatically deduct the money you intend to save toward that goal. If you find that you are overly responsive to your supervisor's wishes at work, find someone in your life who can have regular meetings with you to support other efforts—a spiritual adviser, an artistic mentor, someone whose presence in your life can counterbalance the emotional presence of your supervisor. Experiment with finding different kinds of support and protection for your longer-term goals.

When things don't go as planned—and they won't, always—make adjustments as you go, with kindness toward yourself. Sometimes when I do my portfolio review, I realize that I have not been a world-class father lately: I've been traveling a lot, distracted by new projects, tired, and grumpy. There is an opportunity then for me to feel awful about myself—I'm a bad father, and so on—but it's much better for everyone if I say, All right, I was just an okay father this month, so next month I'm going to plan more family days.

when there just isn't time

There is a limit, though, to how much you can achieve with better emotional support and more careful time management. For many of us, it often seems that we simply lack the capacity to do what we want to do. We have plans, we have dreams, we may even have supportive friends or family, but then the hours fill and life happens—and years go by. The only cure for that is to get back to basic creativizing and emptying the bag. The most important question for rebalancing your portfolio life may well be: What can you stop? And the difficulty, as much as anything, is to see the *opportunity* to stop.

If you talk to parents with one child, they will tell you almost universally that they had no idea how much extra time they had in their lives until they had a child and that time went away. Then if you talk to people with two children, they will say the equivalent thing about their own situation—that they had so much free time they didn't appreciate before they had a *second* child. And those with three children will say the same thing about the days when there were only two, and on it goes. So how do we find that hidden time that, it seems, we can't see until we lose it?

The answer is to return to the portfolio life exercise and ask of every commitment: Could I do less of this? Many of our small commitments are only habits left over from previous versions of our portfolios. Caroline, for example, was naturally comfortable as a red or Control innovator in real estate, and she developed many small systems and touches for preparing houses she was trying to sell. Early in her career that helped establish her reputation, but long after she was in demand as a Realtor, she went on doing many small tasks that were no longer necessary or that she could have handed off to an assistant.

Many of our commitments are out of date. We do things for our children or our parents or friends that they have long since learned to do for themselves—or could learn to do, with a little encouragement. We rescue those who can take care of themselves. We still pay our bills by hand when a computer could do most of the work for us; we check our email constantly when we are at home, even though our lives don't actually require us to be on-call every day around the clock.

If you feel you don't have the capacity—the time, energy, and other resources in your life—to do the things that matter most, then a "capacity review" should be part of every portfolio review you do. That means looking hard at the questions: What can I do less? What can I hand off to someone else? What can I stop entirely?

Set targets for the amount of capacity you want to increase. Could you free up two hours, twice a week? Then try for more in your next life portfolio review. Experiment with different ways to make those cuts. I have a friend who discovered that he felt better after a twenty-minute nap than after hours of flipping through magazines, surfing the Net, and otherwise "relaxing." The discovery changed his approach to weekends. I have another friend, a sculptor, who felt happier after two weeks working at an artist's colony than after a conventional vacation in Europe. I am not saying that you should be stricter with yourself and work harder. I'm saying that the only thing that matters is that you feel energized and renewed, and it may require some innovation in order to find what does that for you at this new time in your life. Once you find more activities that renew you, and once you cut out more of the unsatisfying time and commitments you don't actually need to keep, you will have a greater capacity to attend to the parts of your portfolio you value most.

chapter thirty-six

THE GIFT

About ten years ago I lost an argument with my dad. It was an argument about innovation—specifically, about what he should do with the rest of his life. My dad was always a very competitive guy: a state champion running the half mile and a member of a world-record mile relay team. The regret of his life was that he missed joining the 1956 Olympics team—by one second. He went to college, but my parents had a lot of young kids and he never graduated. So he worked in a factory, rising to the level of committee man (negotiator) in the Allied Industrial Workers Union. He always went to see all of his kids' sporting events.

After he had spent twenty-four years and nine months at the factory, just shy of his twenty-five-year vesting, the company decided to move the plant to Tennessee. Stuck at half-pension, he took a job working for a pest control company, spraying for bugs. At this point I was in graduate school, working on my PhD. I thought I knew how the story should go from here. I sent away for his college transcripts. I looked over the transcripts and the old college catalog and then I called the bursar and asked: Do you realize what your school has done? According to your catalog, this man should have a degree. He could have had a different life! And the bursar hemmed and hawed, but one day an envelope showed up for my dad with a degree inside.

Now he had his degree and he was only in his fifties. I was ex-pecting he would do something with the degree, but he didn't. He continued to work in pest control. It turned out that what he really wanted was to be a coach. Lacking any previous background in coaching, he couldn't get a men's track team, but he got a position coaching women's track. His team started producing great runners—international quality. He loved doing it. For a decade he was well satisfied with his life.

Now he was feeling older and he retired from coaching. But as soon as he quit coaching, he became very involved in helping to raise his grandchildren. He spent whole days with them. He was the go-to grandparent for babysitting. This was when we had the argument. I said, "Dad, you need to stop taking on everybody's work. You're working really hard looking after all these grandkids. You ought to take it easier."

He wasn't having any of that. He said, "This is what I love to do. I always wanted to develop people, to get them to be champions. It gets me out of bed every day and who are you to tell me I shouldn't be doing it?" It hadn't occurred to me until then that he'd innovated a new way to keep being a coach. I said, "You know what? I'm wrong. You're right."

As it turns out, the research is on his side. A study in *BMJ* (what used to be called *The British Medical Journal*) found that people live longer when they retire *later.* In the study, even when the researchers accounted for other factors such as gender and socioeconomic status, people who retired at fifty-five were almost twice as likely to die in the first ten years after retirement as those who kept working. I think this is what my father knew intuitively about innovation: When you stop trying to become new and improved, when you view retire-ment or anything else as the end goal of your life, then you no longer have anything pulling you forward. You lose your essential motiva-tion to grow.

The non-innovator thinks: I may have problems today or things

I lack, but I'm going to solve them and one day I'll get "there"—success, retirement, whatever the goal—and then everything will work perfectly and I'll feel complete and happy. But the innovator thinks: I have problems and challenges and opportunities today, and that will always be true. I'll never get "there." No one will. The weather keeps changing and so do our communities and each one of us, individually. One day, the fishing spot that we relied on for decades—why move your boat when you're catching fish every day?—will lose its magic. Marshall McLuhan's last principle of innovation was that over time, innovation reverses into its opposite: The automobile that promised speed and freedom gives rise to the freeway but also the traffic jam. Email, which promised to speed up our lives and free us from waiting by the mailbox, now monopolizes what used to be our free time. What starts as a new solution becomes the new problem. So we must start experimenting again.

Even when we achieve our goals, we still find that wholeness is not a destination, it's an aspiration. It's always out there ahead of us. We are never perfectly finished, perfectly whole. And that's hard, isn't it? It's hard because we're always going to feel at least a little incomplete. *But it's also a gift.* The gift is that our incompleteness pulls us onward, advances us into the future.

The innovator discovers that life is not a race in a straight line from here to the finish, but instead an ongoing series of overlapping cycles. And while those cycles have predictable stages, those stages don't come according to the calendar. We may associate the Create approach with young people starting out, but our brains are capable of creativity at every age; every life transitions back to green at times. Lately, we are seeing a boom in women going back to work late and becoming entrepreneurs: Some studies find that as many as 70 percent of new companies in the United States are being started by women. At the same time, I notice that increasingly I meet retired factory workers or executives working in "people" jobs—driving for a car service or making the coffee drinks at a café. Some of them don't even need the money, but they find they are still compelled to be out in the world, talking to smart and interesting people, just as they always were. Perhaps the greatest example of a life of ongoing innovation was that of Ben Franklin, who at different times was an author, printer, politician, postmaster, scientist, inventor, activist, statesman, and diplomat. He was not a perfect man—for example, he wasn't much of a husband or father—but like all the innovators I have mentioned, he learned to reinvent himself for each new phase of his life. All of these people are innovators. And I admire them all.

We start out trying to hit this target or that target, but in the end our experiments, experiences, and reflections change us. As we try new approaches, our trying makes us wiser and better. So while the non-innovator wishes to innovate once and be finished, the true innovator discovers that if we innovate well, we still have problems, but they are more manageable; we still have challenges, but they are more interesting and rewarding; we never "get there," but as we master the four steps to innovation, we create the understanding and the tools to remake ourselves anew for each situation and each phase of life. This is the true gift: to see that by our nature we are incomplete, and exactly because we are incomplete we rise in the morning with purpose and drive and the possibility of greatness. We get to become new and improved from here on out.

appendix

INSTRUCTIONS FOR
THE *INNOVATION YOU* ASSESSMENT

iYou mini assessment

1. Think about a particular innovation challenge you would like to undertake.
2. For each question, put the number 1 next to the option that represents the best reponse (the most applicable to you).
3. Complete all three sections for your personal, communal, and universal profile.

section 1. personal

I AM:

___ Supportive

___ Imaginative

___ Competitive

___ Productive

I FACE CHALLENGES BY:

___ Asking for advice

___ Developing novel solutions

___ Taking charge

___ Getting the facts

I AM ENERGIZED BY:

___ Working with people

___ Generating new ideas

___ Delivering results

___ Optimizing systems

section 2: communal

THIS COMMUNITY IS:

___ Cooperative

___ Creative

___ Assertive

___ Efficient

THEY FACE CHALLENGES BY:

___ Communicating with each other

___ Trying different solutions

___ Executing the plan

___ Analyzing the problem

WHAT THEY DO BEST IS:

___ Consider diverse viewpoints

___ Come up with new ideas

___ Overcome specific challenges

___ Work efficiently

section 3: universal

THESE CONDITIONS FAVOR THINGS THAT ARE DONE:

___ Together

___ First

___ Fast

___ Right

THE ENVIRONMENT ENCOURAGES:

___ Long-term development

___ Breakthrough performance

___ Short-term performance

___ Incremental advancement

THE CURRENT CONTEXT REWARDS:

___ Diplomacy

___ Foresight

___ Action

___ Discipline

how to calculate your results:

For each section, use Table 1 to add all the A's, B's, C's, and D's.

Table 1. Calculate your assessment

SECTION 1: PERSONAL			
Choice	A	B	C	D
Question #1				
Question #2				
Question #3				
Section 1 Total				

SECTION 2: COMMUNAL			
Choice	A	B	C	D
Question #1				
Question #2				
Question #3				
Section 2 Total				

SECTION 3: UNIVERSAL			
Choice	A	B	C	D
Question #1				
Question #2				
Question #3				
Section 3 Total				

Example: See Table 2 for Jane Smith's assessment results.

Table 2. Jane Smith's Assessment Results

SECTION 1: PERSONAL			
Choice	A	B	C	D
Question #1				1
Question #2			1	
Question #3				1
Section 1 Total	**0**	**0**	**1**	**2**

SECTION 2: COMMUNAL			
Choice	A	B	C	D
Question #1				1
Question #2				1
Question #3	1			
Section 2 Total	**1**	**0**	**0**	**2**

SECTION 3: UNIVERSAL			
Choice	A	B	C	D
Question #1	1			
Question #2	1			
Question #3	1			
Section 3 Total	**3**	0	0	0

how to interpret your profile:

1. Section 1 represents your personal innovation approach.
2. Section 2 represents your community's innovation approach.
3. Section 3 represents the situation or context of your innovation challenge.
4. For each section, the highest total represents the dominant innovation approach.
    a. If your highest total is in column A, then the innovation approach is "Collaborate."
    b. If your highest total is in column B, then the innovation approach is "Create."
    c. If your highest total is in column C, then the innovation approach is "Compete."
    d. If your highest total is in column D, then the innovation approach is "Control."
5. In the event that there is a tie, the choice in question 1 wins. For instance, you have a tie between choice A (question 1), C (question 3), and D (question 2) in your personal profile, then choice A wins and thus your personal approach is "Collaborate."

For example,

1. Jane Smith's personal innovation approach is "Control."
2. Jane Smith's community's innovation approach is "Control."
3. Jane Smith's situation advocates an innovation approach that is "Collaborate."

More information on working with the Innovation You Assessment can be found at www.innovationyou.com.

about the author

JEFF DEGRAFF, PH.D., is a clinical professor at the Ross School of Business at the University of Michigan and the executive director of Innovatrium, a leading creativity center for executives. He is a consultant to the world's most prominent companies (from Apple to Visa), serves as an adviser to think tanks and governments, and is the author of three business books and numerous articles. Dubbed "the Dean of Innovation" because of his influence in the field, and featured on public television's *Innovation You with Dr. Jeff DeGraff*, he lives in Ann Arbor, Michigan. Visit his website, www.jeffdegraff.com or www .innovationyou.com.

about the type

The text of this book was set on the Monotype in a type-face called Bell. The Englishman John Bell (1745–1831) was responsible for the original cutting of this design. The vocations of Bell were many—among others, book-seller, printer, publisher, type founder, and journalist. His types were considerably influenced by the delicacy and beauty of the French copper-plate engravers. Monotype Bell might also be classified as a delicate and refined rendering of Scotch Roman.